Dedicated to my mother and father

These people do not endorse or share my views or opinions but I do want to acknowledge them

Johnny "went a court'n" Vanore; Lisa aka Alaska, the rock and roller; The Zoucha brothers; Big Steve Strapic; Omar G; Shannon; Mark Rice (Jarhead Extraordinaire); Cyrus the Turk and "EL-A-NORE" : *Thank you all! For your encouragement…by pretending to take me seriously, you are all "friendship" in the consummate.*

Sira and Cliff Weaver- who believe in the "right-to-life" so much they adopted two children, one from a soviet orphanage and the other from China. And speaking of adoption let me mention my cousin Japa Kaur and her husband Harpal who adopted a little Dakota Indian boy and Tim and Careth Daly whom have also adopted children and they issue that same challenge to the rest of you who proclaim yourselves to be pro-life. *"Childbirth is an act of nature…adoption is an act of GOD" ~ Unknown*

To my Aunt Diane for your service and my Grandfather, a proud union man for General Motors, drove a Chevrolet till the day he died and probably still is…

To my high school football coaches Pete Piccarillo and Gil Muscattello who taught me on the football field and in life, "if you are not dishing out, you are taking it."

i

"A man can never die as long as his name is spoken"

Steven Quarno, Pete Carroll, Joseph Masituka, Russell Barnes, John Robinson, Mike and Joan Mottola, Dennis Murray Sr, Oliver Murnane, Donald "Buddy" Hall -WWII Marine Pacific Theater, Brian Daly, Charles Ranor, Philly Marchase, Helen Mulligan, John Knowles, Billy Gregor, Mark Matwick, Fred "the cooler" Stone, NC State LB legend! Peter Hicks, Cable Bob, David Weaver IV, Pat Krolak, Dr. Lynn Stevens, Charles " The Fess" Fessenden, Gary "Snappy" Kelly, David Laudani, Joel Preston, Stephen Strapic Sr, Eric Gomez, Dave Weissman, and Mr. Coors, Later!

Table of Contents

Forward

Disclaimer: *This was written with no affiliation or endorsement to any political party or their agenda. I say this because although I have never been a member, throughout the book I reference unions, and I do not want the inference I am aligning with a known pro-union party.*

While both parties aim to salvage the country in their own way, I fail to understand why they continue to thrive? The Republicans are divided between god, guns and oligarchs, and the liberal Democrats are divided on all their agendas. Personally, I think liberalism is inversely proportional to reality. I feel that anyone who steps forward as an Independent would be embraced for no other reason it gives them credence by stating "see, I'm not even going to try and bullshit you with party unity."

I mention the criticism above because what I write about transcends the two parties. The problem is that more and more decisions are being made today with the axiom, "I'm only doing what my data or software tells me to do." It is an unintended consequence of the "digital age" and why you will see me mention the unions as an effort to introduce some pragmatism back into the economic equation.

Without some type of action, I believe our democracy is moving past the peak on the distribution bell curve and we are beginning to see the signs of an oligarchy. We have successfully filed a lawsuit against American Airlines for bringing down the World Trade Center: to me an act of treason. Another is the marketing "for profit" business off of wounded and dead military or sick and dying children. Regardless of your intentions, it is unacceptable to line your pockets off the pain and anguish of your fellow Americans; make a donation! And personally, I find having to watch commercials openly stating "for an erection lasting longer than four hours" with my grandmother as a sure sign someone has way too much authority and is "dictating" to the masses.

I have to be careful, though, because any slight on democracy or "capitalism" can be easily spun into who knows what label? So let me say how much I love and respect my country and will gladly defend it with my life...again! If anyone wants to label me I would prefer "Veteran" and an American exercising the privileges afforded to him by the blood and sacrifice of all those who have died defending and protecting our Constitution, and whose last breath waves the flag that we live under. I am proud to be an American.

Despite the Declaration of Independence, our democracy was also founded on the belief that men are not inherently "good." We are innately greedy and selfish. Despite initial good intentions, we will always try to seize power and subjugate those who we perceive to be weaker. It is the history of mankind and exactly why we have established the judicial, legislative and executive branches. All three! So two are always keeping one in "check" essentially saying "we don't trust you" and "well we don't trust you" and "we don't trust you either" and it works! Another outstanding example of the founding fathers understanding of human nature or how to maintain a "balance" of power is the military answering to layers of civilian authority. The president, the secretary of defense, the secretaries and the assistant secretaries of Navy, Army, and Air Force all by design the general's answer to civilians. So as you can see in their noble endeavor of creating our democracy, the forefathers knew avarice and tyranny are ubiquitous and had the foresight to address these flaws accordingly.

In 1776 the currency was loyalty, an intangible that fostered the birth of our nation. It was the wealth that was exchanged and it gave you power over your environment, sustained your family and was available to all who came and settled. Now our currency is the dollar and the selfie that gives us power and control over all of our lives.

Today, money and power are synonymous, and the two are slowly drifting into the hands of a select few, subsequently dividing us further as a nation. It is no secret we have a diminishing middle class. Nick Hanauer, a venture capitalist, eloquently explained how and why this is happening in his recent essay appropriately titled, "Why the middle class can't get ahead."

He cites: From the 1950s-1980s the great middle class was created, corporate profits averaged a healthy 6 percent of GDP; but now it has doubled to more than 12 percent of GDP. Those extra trillion dollars is profit because powerful people like me prefer it to be. It could have been spent on your wages, but capitalists like me are growing wealthy beyond our parents' wildest dreams because of your misfortune.

Mr. Hanauer should be commended for his honesty. It is a rare quality today, especially coming from someone of his stature, and he has my respect. That being said, his article reads almost like a confession. But as he points out under a thriving population of corporate oligarchs and I would add tort attorneys, middle class wealth is being usurped. If for no other reason it is the only available source to be plundered, and let me elaborate on the "how" as it relates to my story. The most significant is through "compulsory" participation in the "digital" or virtual economy specifically as employees or skilled workers. Another is your credit score, which they own and holds more power than your vote. Last, we see an exodus of regulatory agents into the private finance sector. A move I doubt would win approval from the founding fathers as it's a recipe for tyranny and why the stock market will crash again. It is under these assertions along with Mr. Hanauer's affirmation that I keep coming back to the idea of unions as way to protect both workers and consumers or the middle class. I believe I can speak for the many when I say as achievers and people who take pride in an "honest day's tangible work," no one is looking for a hand out. But I feel that other than armed rebellion the unions offer us our only protection from becoming a two-class society.

On a whim, I had recently joined workers4unions on social media and shortly thereafter posted "Unions create a middle class." This started a firestorm of comments, but more importantly I realized I was not alone. I like to think of a unionized labor force as a form of "check and balance" in the private sector. I would say the North Western University men's football team agrees with me, and I address the argument for unions in the chapter aptly titled: A Call to Union.

You will see my story is divided into two sections. The first part is a little bit about my life, so that you can see where I am coming from. My history is not unlike most Americans: a desire to find my niche in life and my journey to get there. Like most, I had hills, valleys, and a few tangents off–the-beaten path, but as one of my favorite aphorisms go. *"There will be two dates on your tombstone, but all that really matters is that little 'dash' between them."*
The bulk of the book is unedited excerpts from my journal as I documented two years of my life as a cellular field tech. It is definitely a story as told by a grunt in the trenches, who had to deal with a myriad of abstract processes, management on meds, workforce software,

codes and more processes; did I say processes? The important thing to remember is that while my examples are from the telecom industry, I believe they are applicable to all sectors of the economy and to anyone who considers themselves to be a "contributing employee" of our democracy.

As you read I may come across as a malcontent, but please keep this in mind. If someone didn't say "sleeping on this cave floor sucks" we'd still be there. And if someone didn't say "man, this king is a fucking asshole"...we would still be an English colony. I see the glass as half empty, because I want to see it full.

While dated with time stamps there is no chronological order as these are just excerpts related to topics. My book also includes some funny anecdotes along with social commentary, and some very personal experiences. It is a catharsis and my reflection on how "for the people by the people" has evolved into "Iam-the-capitalist-pig-sucking-the-oasis-of-america-dry.com" An overall expression of my disillusionment in what I believe many of us were brought up to aspire to. All while "quantified" and integrated into the "corporate matrix." Enjoy!

Note: All correspondence has been edited to comply with confidentiality and non-disclosure agreements, and all names have been changed. Any similarity is pure coincidence. Some company names are factious specifically the two I speak of most often while I was writing my journal. You will also see the use of numbers as code for letters along with some redactions and dates for the year 1999; all for legal purposes. Everything else you read is based on my personal observations, not judgments. Simply put "I don't judge, I observe."

The five words most spoken to a man in a suit:

"Will the Defendant Please Rise"

Chapter 1

Beginnings

It is funny as you look back on life and see the various paths your journey takes and how it leads to what you do as an adult. Some people seem to go straight from point A to point B. My road from A to B was anything but a straight line. I like to think it's more like Roberts Frost's poem with a slight spin the "roads"…less traveled.

I was born in Chicago, Illinois in 1962, a month before the Cuban missile crisis. My birth had no bearing on the event, but as amateur historian, it fascinates me how close we were to almost exterminating ourselves as a species. A good part of my infant life was being an international football getting punted around Europe with my mom and dad. That's because my parents met in Plano, Texas in the mid-1950s. It was the "golden age of flight" and my father was a fighter pilot in the Air Force flying the legendary F-86 Sabre. Mom was a flight attendant with American Airlines or more specifically a "stewardess" as they were called at the time.

Eventually my parents ended up in Istanbul, Turkey, where my father was stationed. Dad no longer on flight status was a courier officer. He would disappear for days picking up Intel from listening posts around the Black Sea and traveling to bases in Afghanistan and Pakistan, all part of the cold war spying on the Soviets. My mother said she could not bear to hear a Turkish doctor while giving birth, so my dad sent her back to her home of Chicago to have me. Soon we rejoined my father overseas and lived all over

Europe; apparently Italian doctors were more acceptable as my brother was born in Rome. While there she also shook hands with JFK. He had stopped at the ambassador's residence and was in route to Germany to deliver his famous "Ich-bin-ein-Berliner" speech. Dad still on active duty with the Air Force when we finally moved back to the states and briefly settled in Tacoma, Washington where he did a brief stint in Vietnam.

Soon enough my father stepped down from active duty, but he stayed active with the Air Force Reserve. He decided it was time to make his mark in civilian life and to accomplish that he would need to his degree. One of my first memories of my dad is when he said he was going to attend college. He packed up the family and we moved to Silver Spring, Maryland, where he attended the University of Maryland at College Park. We were there four years until he graduated in the new field of Information Systems.

This enabled him to secure a job at the corporate giant Johnson & Johnson. My dad proved as successful in the corporate world as he was in the military, and he steadily rose through the ranks at the pharmaceutical colossus. It was from him and my mother I was exposed to the corporate environment. I can still hear my mother using "corporate" as an adjective to describe someone or, more often, to describe what they were lacking.

It is anyone's guess how far my father could have ascended in the hierarchy of Johnson & Johnson. Tragically, prostate cancer would take him way too early. His passing wreaked havoc on our family. It's been 31 years and now and then I look at my picture of him standing next to his jet, I still tear up.

New Jersey

When Johnson & Johnson came calling, I was in the third grade and we moved to New Jersey. I was a terrible student growing up and it frustrated my parents to no end. As a young kid I remember being interested in everything around me, except for the books in front of me. I was a typical little boy who couldn't sit still. I am sure by today's standards I would have been diagnosed with Attention Deficit Disorder and they would have had me on Ritalin or some type of meds.

Those were great days to be growing up. There were lots of kids and we would have neighborhood games in whatever sport was in season: football in the fall, rec league basketball in the winter, and baseball in the spring and summer. We wore tough skin jeans and moms still had to iron patches in the knees; it was great. And with all the children came the parents and their obvious interests in the kids. It struck me as odd, but I remember adults whom I barely knew seemed to take an interest in me. Strangers would approach and congratulate me on a game, or engage me in conversation. There was a real interest in the kids from all the parents, and I always felt welcomed and accepted. The name of my small world was Long Valley N.J. and they made me feel like a rock star. With the advent of social media I have reconnected with childhood friends and it is a testimony to how fortunate I was to have grown up there.

In the spring of fifth grade, I picked up a lacrosse stick and quit baseball. This would be an epic event in my life. It was a sport I became very good at and by my freshman year in high school I started on the varsity. This led to hanging out with high school seniors, some of whom were 18. Back then, at 18, you could legally purchase alcohol. We were typical kids who would get into all kinds of mischief and the easy access to booze didn't hurt. Sometimes we would go into New York City a place called "Hell's Kitchen" to buy beer or drugs, yell at the hookers. Just check out the mayhem. Back then New York was like an apocalyptic movie; instead of zombies there were heroin addicts. All of that has a lot of appeal to a young man exploring the world. Nothing like it is today. Despite my mother's misgivings, I was getting my exposure to the world, and boy was it fun! The implications of growing up in North Jersey really dawned on me when I was in the Marines Corps.

Cold War warrior; my father, he always talked about the "domino theory" call sign "Playboy," next to his F-86 Sabre, Luke AFB AZ, circa 1956, there was no FAA . He said they would fly through the Grand Canyon, buzz commercial airliners, and fly up to Washington State to pick up Olympia beer.

Often, Marines would come through the barracks collecting money for the newly arrived Private Smith, who was a virgin, and had never consumed alcohol. They would get him drunk and buy him an escort. It was all new to him, and eventually he would end up getting kicked out. I used to think *Thank god I'm from Jersey.*

My high school was West Morris Central and our football team was the Wolfpack. "The strength of the wolf is in the pack, and the strength of the pack is in the wolf." I was almost not a graduate of my high school, but it just shows how life works out some time.

I had a good friend on the football team. We both played linebacker; he played middle and I was left, and we were pretty good. His mom ran the lunchroom. Little did I know it would help me to receive my diploma!

In high school, one could receive credits towards graduation for working during study hall, and I had been working in the cafeteria since I was a sophomore. To be honest, credits really weren't on my mind it was the never-ending free buffet. My senior year we could not fit cafeteria work into my class schedule; however, my friend's mother would allow me to go in the back and move milk crates and help out so I could grab a free lunch.

At the end of my senior year I missed a final exam in public speaking and ended up failing the half-year course. I believe I am the only student in the history of my high school with this dubious honor. I had been to the shore, partied all weekend and forgot my final speech was due. By failing the course I was short 2.5 credits I needed to graduate. Needless to say, my parents were beside themselves. This is where others who were looking out for me stepped in.

The next week I was at school picking up a yearbook and looking into summer school. My guidance counselor approached and asked about my work in the lunchroom. He then asked my friend's mother if she thought I was eligible for any credits based on the work I did through the school year. She replied, "I think he helped out enough for 2.5 credits." That was it! I went from zero to graduating high school. On the surface this may seem shallow, but they were helping me. I was bad on the outside, not on the inside. To Mrs. Joan Mottola may you RIP; and Mrs. Mary LaSapio and my Principal Ron Batistoni, please know you have my eternal and deepest gratitude.

Looking back I was really a scared kid. My small rock star life was coming to an end. Remember, I was a terrible student, but not a terrible person. Make no mistake-- I grew up in a loving home, but I was told at an early age: "We love you, but when you turn 18, you are either in college or you're out." To be honest, I heard it more from my mother.

Despite my academic record, I was invited to visit a few small colleges for both football and lacrosse. I had received all-state honors in both sports, most notably in lacrosse. Eventually, I was recruited to the local junior college by the lacrosse coach. Athletics was a huge part of my life. It was all I knew. To be honest, academics were secondary, and sports and the parties after were first. When the local junior college coach approached me, I enrolled and was playing the next spring. It turned out he had recruited players from some of my rival high schools all around North Jersey. Many of whom I played against and we all knew of each other. Without a doubt we had a great team and we all became fast friends. If I recall, in my second year we only lost one game. Junior college was a way to keep playing lacrosse, chip away at school, and possibly get recruited; at least that was the idea.

During lacrosse season in the spring, I was enrolled full-time and in the fall I would take a lighter class load and work.

13

I had made some connections with some big-time drug traffickers. They owned stash houses all over North Jersey and in eastern Pennsylvania, and they would pay me to maintain them. Another job I had was to hand dig and burlap trees for a local nursery as well as work for Mayflower movers, so I am not afraid of hard work. I was always working in some capacity. It was just academics I had difficulty muddling through. I got through my basic freshman courses and knew my credits could eventually transfer to a four-year school, but I found myself once again floundering as a recreation major! As I was getting close to the fall of my second year, I mentioned to my father I was thinking of taking the semester off. Well, he hit the roof! I will never forget it. He said, "I want rent! You get your own car insurance! You are going to start working full-time!"

I don't know why but for some reason the car insurance thing scared the shit out of me. Maybe it was because I had no idea how to get it? I think not going to school and the fact I was currently involved in a law suit, was a determining factor for him. You see, I had been involved in an altercation where someone had jumped out of a car and took a swing at me with a baseball bat. I'm sure people who have been in combat can relate, but there is an inner rage that is indescribable when you think someone is trying to take your life. All I remember is people pulling me off of him. Yup, somebody takes a swing at me and then sues me when I defend myself.

I had bought some time but as time does, it was running out. And it was running out for both my father and me. He was 47 and had been diagnosed with prostate cancer. I remember him coming to my lacrosse games on crutches, but the seriousness just never registered. I was oblivious to my father fighting for his life and it haunts me to this very day. All I can say is I was a young man desperately struggling to find himself. I was under enormous pressure from my parents and my peers to do something with my life. People were moving on. I had three younger brothers and I could not stay at home anymore. Yet, I had no clue as to what I was going to do or where I was even going.

I heard one of my friends had joined the Navy. Ever with the competitive nature, I would go one better: I would join the Marine Corps!

The Corp (Semper Fi)

After my father had laid down the law, I went to see the recruiter. Enlisting in the service seemed like a good solution. Again, I was thinking it would buy me some time. For what – who knows? I found out years later my mom was calling the recruiter. To quote her, she told him, "Come get him. Strike while the iron is hot!" Of course, I thought basic training would be like football camp, and naturally I would do well. Not exactly!

People get a kick out of this story and it really happened. I grew up wearing "tighty whities" with the label to the back side. In boot camp they issue you boxers for underwear with the label in front over the open fly. Whenever a drill instructor would enter the squad bay he would bark "ON LINE!" You dropped whatever you were doing and jumped on a line in front of your bunk, standing at attention just like in the movie Full Metal Jacket. I just got out of the shower and Sergeant Slate, a large, dark green Marine, whose name conjures up everything you can imagine for a Marine Corps drill instructor, came in and barked "ON LINE!" I instinctively grabbed my skivvies and jumped on line standing at attention looking straight ahead; locked and cocked. He came walking down the squad bay eying us up and down and then suddenly starts coming right towards me.

15

He walks up and puts the brim of his Smoky Bear hat on the bridge of my nose. He looks me dead in the eye and snarls *"Are we expecting company tonight?"* In my haste I had put my boxers on backwards, and the label and open fly to my rear end! I could see he was about to burst out laughing. He barked "Fix it NOW, EE-leven!" That was my number eleven. "Sir, yes sir!" I yelled and turned my boxers around. The laughs on me!

I went in the Marines determined to get some training or marketable skill. I remember my dad telling me, "Son, you don't want to be cannon fodder." I was thinking electronics was a good move, so I could become an electrician. I scored high enough on the aptitude tests to go to aviation electronics school. I spent about eight months stationed just outside of Memphis, Tennessee in the most intense curriculum you can imagine. At the end of each section it was mandatory to pass a test with a perfect score. You would get three chances after that you went to see the gunny. In the eyes of the Marine Corps, if you flunk out then "YOU" just broke your contract! The Corps could do with you whatever they wanted; the gunny reminded you of this. I ended up going once; as usual school was a real struggle for me.

Guys would "rock out" as it was called and you knew this because their chairs would be turned upside down on their desk when you came in the next morning. The instructors did this to fuck with your head. I made it through electronics school and would eventually become a designated air crew drawing flight pay and logging close to a 50 hours air time on the CH-46 helicopter. I was meritoriously promoted to NCO (Non-Commissioned Officer) and deployed with the 24th MAU (Marine Amphibious Unit) on board the Helicopter Assault Ship, *LPH Guam*. I traveled all over the East Coast, and flew all around the Mediterranean including the renowned Amalfi coast from Naples down to Sicily. I even managed to get a buddy to sign me back on the ship from liberty so I could stay out in town with a French girl I had meet while in Toulon. If I had gotten caught I would have been UA (Unauthorized Absence) and in big trouble but it was the last port of our deployment and I was going to be discharged when we got back. I figured what the hell; it would make for a good story someday if I ever wrote a book.

On the 50 doing gun runs, the most fun you can have with clothes on. Thanks to my dad taking me to the range as a kid, I had also qualified as a Rifle Expert with the M16 and was a range coach for my helicopter squadron.

I have mixed emotions about the Marine Corps. I am very proud of my service and wish I saw combat although I'm not sure how well I would do with ROE's (rules of engagement). In my opinion the battlefield is not the place to practice law because as we all know…justice is blind. I believe ROE's undermine autonomy and creates an air dissent because it implies "we don't trust you." I mean, we're the good guys, right?

When terrorists blew the barracks up in Beirut, I was stationed in California and I remember thinking, *this is it! This is the modern equivalent of Pearl Harbor. We're going to war!* And then we left. Nothing! All those lives wasted and that's blood on Ronald Reagan's hands. The Marines were operating under Rules of Engagement and as peace keepers? Marines are not peace keepers, Marines are peace makers! I could hear my father's words about "cannon fodder." I knew I was getting out.

Years later, when I was starting college, I ran into a buddy from my squadron in town for the weekend. He was getting ready to be discharged and told me about a conversation with one of our maintenance chiefs "top" Smith. "Top" is Marine Corps jargon for a senior enlisted man; just picture an arm full of stripes. My friend said Top Smith told him "the good ones get out" specifically naming me and a couple of my friends. I took it as a compliment. In all the Marine Corps was the best mistake I ever made, but I had aspirations of graduating from college. By now my father had passed away from cancer, and it was something my parents had always wanted me to do.

College

There are not enough words to express the elation and feeling of freedom when you are getting "released" from active duty. Folks in prison are probably the same way – they count down to their "release" date. But there is a great deal of adjustment coming off of active duty. It is called "civil readjustment" and it was mandatory to attend lectures about returning to civilian life before getting out. The intensity of being an active duty Marine for four years and being deployed in the FMF (Fleet Marine Force) was unbelievable. I still carry a little bit of it with me to this very day.

A friend I grew up with in New Jersey was playing lacrosse at the University of North Carolina at Chapel Hill. I had previously visited him on several occasions. In fact, it was his father who had brought the sport to our town and started our youth league, introducing me to the sport when I was in the fifth grade.

When I had visited the university in the past I remember being in complete awe of the campus and the students. Growing up, I was made to think the only way to attend an institution of this reputation was to be of a royal bloodline... or at the very least a valedictorian. But here was a neighborhood friend, my goalie in high school and junior college, now at this prestigious Division I school. Maybe these people were mere mortals! When I was discharged from the Marines he had invited me to come up, so I did.

My friend's eligibility to play lacrosse was up, but he was completing his last few courses and would graduate in the spring, and was thinking of graduate school. I was re-adjusting to civilian life by taking in all the sites on campus. He said he had heard of a very good lacrosse club at NC State, which was just down the road in Raleigh. The university had recently dropped their program due to team disciplinary problems; go figure? Apparently, there were still some players who stuck around instead of transferring out so they had a pretty talented team. We contacted the president of the club and arranged a meeting.

We met with him and he told us he was also president of the hockey club as well as majoring in electrical engineering.

His accomplishments were making me feel intimidated again. He was very friendly and said we were more than welcome to join. That spring we lived in Chapel Hill, but came daily to Raleigh for practices. Coming out of the Corps, I was in excellent condition and had no problem running with the slightly younger crowd. By the end of the season we had made a lot of friends. I am proud to say I am still in contact with some of them to this day. We also hung out with the woman's team, so it added to the whole experience. For a 24 year old fresh out of the Marine Corps, I was having a blast. Cracks were forming in my walls of perception, and maybe I could go to school here?

Many of our new friends were looking for sub-leases for the summer, so finding a place to live was no problem. We packed up and moved to Raleigh. Little did I know I would be there for the next 17 years!

Chapter 2

Another Wolfpack and the Corporate Shuffle

L ife was fun in Raleigh, North Carolina. I enjoyed playing club lacrosse for the NC State Wolfpack. I did whatever I needed to do to pay the bills. I did a brief stint waiting tables and still have friends from the experience. A tornado came through one summer, so I picked up work as a roofer and managed to fall through; fortunately, I did not get hurt. I also had friend who hooked me up with a part time job doing airport maintenance and we even painted lines on the runways.

I had been contemplating taking a course at the university and one of my teammates persuaded me to sign up. I recall I had to enroll at the continuing education building named the McKimmon Center. The Center was symbolic to me because I vividly remember it was located across the street from the main campus and I thought, *OK, this is where I have to attend classes. Part-time students are 'not worthy' ...until admitted as full-time. Then I will be allowed to attend class with the regular full-time students.* It's funny now but this was how much I felt intimated. Remember, I always struggled with academics, so imagine my surprise when I signed up and found out I could take a course with a lacrosse buddy. It was a communications course. The class was an elective for him, but a huge start for me.

Remember, I was a kid who got out of high school by working in the lunchroom. Now I was hanging out with engineering majors. Some were from very prestigious private schools well-known throughout the lacrosse community. I was beaming with pride.

In the beginning, it was almost overwhelming for me. I had to juggle the finances and living accommodations and see if I could really handle the academics. When I finally decided to look into an undergraduate degree, I met with an admissions counselor. I explained my situation and as expected he said, "You will have to take some more courses before you can be admitted as a full-time undergrad."

Fortunately, all of my junior college credits from before my Marine days were accepted by NC State, so I found myself one or two classes short of being a sophomore. With the communications course under my belt, I completed an economics class and re-applied as a political science major. I was admitted! I had no idea what a political science major did, but I knew I was not cut out for engineering. My thinking at the time was I would go into teaching and coaching as there were a lot of history courses in the curriculum and that interested me. But I had a long way to go, and I still had a lot of self-doubt nagging at me. On the other hand, I was an admitted undergraduate and even more thrilling...I am now allowed to mix with the full-time student body (wink, wink).

Yes, I was an undergrad in a great university, but it did not make school any easier for me. As usual, I struggled with my academics. "Two-O and go" was the saying. I had taken out student loans, so quitting was not an option! I also had been through too much in my young life to throw away this opportunity. One thing I did do to ease the course load was attend all the summer sessions. There were two back-to-back, five-week sessions during summer break. You were only allowed to miss one day of any course because class was every day five days a week. Not being your typical student, summers off did not matter to me. In fact, I used to enjoy it because you had the campus and town to yourself. The other important fact was it allowed me to carry a lighter course load and it freed up time for work. I was in school for three straight years until I got my first IT job with only one course left to graduate.

Course Correction

It's funny, but as I was entering my junior year I still wasn't exactly sure what a political scientist did! Fortunately, that question was about to be answered. One of my required courses was Research Methods and Statistics. It was a three-credit course with a one-credit computer lab writing and working with statistical applications such a SAS and SPSS. This turned out to be the class that turned the light on for what would eventually become a career.

In a minute the professor who ran the lab changed my life. I spent a lot of time in the computing lab and I got to know her pretty well. I wish I could say I was there because I was so studious, but the reality is I was there just trying to overcome my fear of computers. But one day as the professor was walking out, she asked, "Ed, can you watch the lab?" To me this meant answer the phone as I have done before and I said "of course" and for no particular reason, except for unsolicited Jersey commentary, I followed with, "Wuddya gottado dageta job round here?"

She looked at me and said, "I have money budgeted for a lab TA (Teaching Assistant). You are hired. I'll talk to you when I get back." My jaw hit the floor. I said, "I was just kidding!"

I remember vividly her exact words to me: "No, no, you'll be fine." When she returned, she hired me. I recall using the DOS "copy" and "delete" commands and thinking *this is just like recording music.* I guess I had a knack for it. She said

23

she watched me helping other students, but I never really thought twice about it.

That's fellow NC State Alum and my friend Van in the pilot seat of Marine One. We were bouncers at a night club together in college. It was a lot of fun and a great way to meet the ladies. He DOES NOT endorse or share my views or opinions nor does President Bush. He is an Iraq War veteran, proud husband/father; and it is my honor to call him a friend. He once sent me a birthday card signed by the president. He now works for World Team Sports http://worldteamsports.org; they organize sporting events for wounded veterans. GO TO THEIR PAGE AND DONATE!

The difficult part about my new position was many of my lacrosse teammates were electrical engineers and computer science majors. They were required to write code so if a monkey banged on the keyboard you would still get a specific output. I had taken an introductory Pascal course in one of my summer sessions, but that was it. Now it seemed like a strange paradox to me. I was working in a computer lab, but I am not a computer science major! It would be different today, but we are talking the early 1990s when the "microcomputer" and "networking" revolution was in its infancy.

I do not want to mislead you. I did not become an instant computer expert who ran the place. There was a lead technician who I worked alongside. Of course, he was an electrical engineering major. My job was to help him and students in the lab. I believe we spent my first summer there building PCs, running co-axial cable throughout the building, and connecting the professors' offices to the new "LAN." My electronics background from the Marine Corps came in handy here.

I finally came to realize this was possibly a career! I applied for a few jobs in the paper and picked up some contract work between school secessions working in RTP. Eventually, I would be working 20 hours for the college of humanities lab where I started, and 20 hours for the university computing center working all over campus. It was tough because I needed all of this experience, but I also had to maintain a full course load. If I fell below full-time student status, I would have to start paying back student loans.

I managed to juggle everything pretty well and even bounced at a night club on the weekends. At one point, I needed to pick up a single credit. With the instructor's permission, I enrolled in a graduate level SAS lab and scheduled myself to work at the same time. I was taking the course I needed and getting paid to do it. What a deal!

As I was getting closer to graduation, I had to start thinking about where I wanted to work. I was not sure I could keep my job at the university if I was no longer a student. I started applying for jobs and eventually I received a call for an interview. It was for a contractor position at Glaxo Pharmaceuticals working in their PC shop. The manager was a NC State graduate. He was kind enough to hire me and still allow me to take the one course I needed to graduate. It was a physics course and every Tuesday and Thursday, I would leave work at lunch and go to class. It was the fall of 1992, and in December I received my diploma. I cried because I knew my father would have been very proud. I think my mother was proud, too...as soon as she got over the shock her wandering son was a college graduate.

The Corporate World

Living in Raleigh and going to NC State the place to work was the Research Triangle Park, or RTP. My understanding was its inception came about to feed off the students coming from the three top-notch universities in the area. In a 30-mile radius you had North Carolina State in Raleigh, University of North Carolina in Chapel Hill, and Duke in Durham, hence the "Triangle." To entice companies they offered tax incentives. I believe this was a revolutionary idea at the time and numerous companies like Northern Telecomm, IBM, Glaxo, Burroughs-Wellcome, AT&T, Reichold Chemical, and Becten Diskson, and others settled there; it was a corporate hotbed.

Glaxo was a British pharmaceutical company. I remember hearing about it in college as one of the premier places in RTP. Never in my wildest imagination did I think I would be working there. The halls were made of white marble and the campus was like a palace. My first job was to build and deliver PCs. I recall going to the airport where they maintained the corporate jets. When I went out to their manufacturing facility, I had to don scrubs. I was given access to all their buildings and was always impressed with the sheer opulence of everything. Within a year of working in the PC shop, I inquired about a position in the new Data Comm Group. I had become friendly with them, as they would make the network connections for the PCs we installed.

I made the transfer, and to be honest, I did not hit it off with my new manager. I remember thinking, *She doesn't even have a college degree, how can she work here?* I always had been told you could never get a job in a company like this without a college diploma. Yet here was this woman who in my opinion couldn't manage a cemetery. Fortunately, it was the 1990s and the IT industry was really growing.

After a year, I received a phone call from a gentleman I had done some contract work while I was in college. He was a Project Manager for a new IT consulting firm and wanted to know if I was interested in joining the company. It was for more money and he made the offer right over the phone. Initially, I declined. Despite the pay hike I was thinking, *I should stay at Glaxo; hope to get hired on permanently, work 20 years, and retire. It's what my parents would have done.* This idea was short-lived when I thought of my manager. So within an hour I called him back and accepted his offer.

I had been at Glaxo for two years. His offer changed my ideas about careers and compensation. The only way to move up and make more money was to go to another company. I wrote my resignation letter similar to the organizational announcements posted at the dining facilities.

"It is with deep regret" kicked off my exit letter like I was some big cheese. I guess I was trying to be corporate? When I think about it now, I roll my eyes. But I was dating a former debutante and hanging out with patent attorneys, Duke MBAs, TV ad executives and HR directors. I'm in the thick of "corporate." My friend Winston had played football for Notre Dame on the 1988 national championship team. If I'm hanging out with these people, maybe I turned out all OK? *This is what you do; you climb the ladder, right?*

Software Engineer – Really!?

When I started my new job with the consulting firm, they handed me business cards with my title as "Software Engineer." Remember, I went to school with software engineers. I barely made it through an introductory course on Pascal – a basic computer language. It was a moral dilemma calling myself a software engineer, so I did not. In retrospect, this was my introduction to corporate deceit and operations.

My first project was as a contractor at Northern Telecomm, which was located in RTP right down the road from Glaxo. I was in charge of the shipping and logistics departments as well as a manufacturing facilities networks and servers. I would bounce between them as needed. It was a pretty cool gig. Sometimes I would walk around and think, *Wow, I can't believe I am working here, this is so cool.* Every now and then, I would call my mother and tell her what I was doing. I'm performing a "download" was big IT jargon at the time. She would tell me about her "Wang" word processor. I think it was my way of saying, "See, I am not a loser because I flunked public speaking!"

My biggest challenges were dealing with the corporate processes. Someone would come to me with a problem and I would go fix it. Sometimes I would hear, "You should have them fill out a request form." I'm thinking: *Why?* In the time it would take to go through the official process of requesting me, I would have the problem fixed and that's what I did.

Sometimes I would inadvertently take something down. They were my servers so I might try something I read about in a trade magazine. Tweak some parameters or update firmware. Then my phone would ring, "Hey, we just lost South East logistics section. Can you take a look?" I would tell them Oh wow..."Yeah I'll see what's up with that!" as if I didn't know. Walk back to the server room, undo what I had changed, call down and ask "How about now?" They would be thrilled it was fixed so quickly and ask "what did you do?" I would make something up or throw some technical terms I know they would never understand.

Don't get me wrong; this was not an everyday occurrence; but it's how you grow and learn. I would often say to the managers, "If I am doing my job well, you will never see me. I should be like the Maytag repair man." They were OK with this philosophy. I took pride in keeping my network and servers up 99.9 percent of the time. I would come in on Sundays and perform prescribed maintenance and I made sure I was always available. I did whatever it took!

At some time during my tenure as a contractor at Northern Telecomm, I was pulled into a meeting with the owner of my contracting firm and a couple of managers from NT. To be honest, I was feeling more loyalty to NT because I worked with them on a daily basis. I got to know them personally. Now all of the sudden the owner of the consulting firm shows up and I am supposed to be on his side? We were sitting in this meeting, they were talking about me, and I am listening and following the conversation intently; and I know the next logical statement coming from the owner of my firm will be, "We have people for that!" Instead he blurts out, "We have resources for that!" I was stunned! I am sitting right there next to him and he is talking about me! Why couldn't he say "people" or my name, "Ed"?

This was one sudden dose of the reality of outsourcing. I will never forget how disrespectful that one little comment was. I wanted to say "are you a pimping me out?" It was a real eye opener.

Sometimes I would get pulled off Northern Telecomm to assist on other projects. We did an audit at ████████ in Charlotte. Yes that ████████, the ones who stamped bad securities as AAA low-risk investments and yet somehow are still in business assigning credit ratings? Another project was an SAP rollout for Reichold Chemical to their manufacturing facilities. I spent time in Vancouver, Chattanooga, Kansas City and a few other cities. We would go out a week at a time. Back then they encouraged you to stay the weekend instead of coming back on Friday because airfare was cheaper if you flew back on Sunday and I took advantage of that offer. I remember suggesting we get T-shirts made like you see a band has with concert tour dates and cities.

Somewhere along the line, our office manager resigned. I remember her saying, "You guys have no idea what's going on," and "You're not going to believe it!" For all I knew she was just making up excuses because I thought she just wanted to leave. Everyone handles things differently. We even had a big going away dinner for her at a well-known steakhouse.

To my surprise I knew our waitress from college. I dated her roommate and she dated a friend of mine. Eventually, she would achieve fame for having an alleged affair with

Michael Jordan and unsuccessfully trying to sue him three times for paternity of her child. I saw her name in the news and I can't really say I was all that surprised.

It was not long after I received a call from my manager at the contracting firm (he was not an employee of Northern Telecomm) informing me the owner had been indicted for tax fraud, and it would be in the papers the next day. I cannot say I was completely in shock or aghast at the idea. As you know, I grew up in Jersey where everything is legal as long as you don't get caught; and besides, nobody voluntarily pays their taxes. We only do it out of fear. If he just could've moved the company headquarters offshore, then it would have been OK. Besides, I was still more upset about being called a resource!

Obviously I had to start looking for other employment options. By now, I had friends from college who were working as recruiters in the still growing IT bubble. I sent them my resume and knew it would only be a few weeks before another position came my way. In the meantime, I was still with the consulting firm.

The last project I was involved with was at BCBS of North Carolina. They had partnered their IT with Arthur Andersen. When I arrived at BCBS, I was asked to go over to the Andersen facility and help out. It struck me as odd they were set up "over there," in separate facility, but what did I know? I was also warned they were very difficult to deal with and I thought, *How can that be, they work for you?*

So I show up at the Arthur Andersen facility in the standard IT uniform of the day: tucked in dress shirt with jeans and sneakers. Well, the first woman I ran into gave me a look to freeze water. As I looked around, I saw every guy wore a white pressed dress shirt and was stylishly decked out. The women all wore fancy business attire, and naturally

I looked around for the hot ones. Do not get me wrong. I was a little anxious, but I had some real experience under my belt. I had passed five exams and was in the process of deciding on the sixth and final exam to become a Microsoft Certified System Engineer. I was bringing that to the table so I felt confident. On arrival, I respectfully introduced myself and asked to see the manager I was told to report to.

I go in as any consultant would, and very politely introduce myself, tell him my background; and then respectfully ask him pertinent questions regarding the network. Basic things, like how many users, number of servers, communication room locations, hardware, WAN links and capacity, any special applications? Right off the top he starts to bully me with questions about my skills. It was his demeanor that really caught me off guard: definitely not what I was expecting. It reminded me of a promotion board in the Marines Corps, and I thought it was uncalled for and unprofessional as I was there to help him as an equal. However, I quickly gathered myself and thought *OK, then, bring it. Test my knowledge.* It does not get any bigger then Arthur Andersen, right? He asked me two questions which I nailed immediately and then struggled for a third. That told me all I needed to know.

I ended up doing some limited desktop and network support. I befriended a few people because we had to interact and work together. While I was there I asked technical questions, some to confirm my suspicions. I recall inquiring about token ring LAN speeds and I would get, "Oh? So and so does that." That's not something anyone does! I could see it in their eyes they had no idea what I was talking about, yet this was what they we're brought in for and getting paid to do! I was shocked and amazed because this was the great Arthur Andersen. They dressed really nice, but that was about it. To me it's just proof when it comes to money and work; people with flashy and nice clothes want you to look at them...in the hope you won't see through them. I call it dress for the distraction. I knew it would not be long before I would be leaving BCBS. It was not uncommon to receive unsolicited phone calls asking if I was interested in some position.

I recall once I had two recruiters going almost simultaneously. I was calling each one back every couple of minutes taking bids on my services. Boom times are fun times in the right industry. It was very lucrative and I was enjoying the fruits of my labor; case in point, I was at a friend's pool party and happened to meet a very attractive woman.

Come to find out she was in town from Myrtle Beach to dance at the local gentleman's club. By coincidence I happened to be a gentleman...so it worked out for both of us. We ended up hanging out and eventually I took a trip to Myrtle Beach. When I walked into her house she reached into the closet where there was a stack of Gallery magazines. She handed me one. She was on the cover and she was the centerfold! I danced around her house singing "my angel is a centerfold!"She got a kick out of it. Without sounding pretentious, I had served in the Marines, paid my way and graduated from a good university. I was working 40 hours a week, making good money, bought a house and started saving for retirement. I had pursued "happiness" and caught it! I think the founding fathers would have been proud.

Still dealing with the Arthur Andersen "fashionistas" one of my phone interviews was for a contract System Administrator at IBM. I was very interested in this job for two reasons. One is just the fact it was IBM. The other is the recruiter who was trying to place me was a personal friend from college. I knew I could squeeze him for more money, which I did. He could also fix my drug test or push it out enough so I would test clean. (I never said I was an angel.) Eventually, I got the IBM offer and accepted the job.

I had been working with Arthur Andersen for a couple of months when I walked in and told them I was taking a position at IBM. It gave me great satisfaction and I could see looks of approval, plus reactions of surprise and envy; surprised because I wore jeans and still got the job. Although it was brief, I just felt really good about myself having stood toe-to-toe with Arthur Andersen; and for the record I didn't intend for it to be that way. It seemed they were more preoccupied with trying to frustrate me and make me look bad instead of working together to help BCBS. It was very disappointing. In my opinion the only function they served was to drive up your health insurance premiums, and I believe the Enron debacle and their subsequent demise validates that thought.

IBM – The Mother Ship

The contract with IBM was at a company called Qualex, now defunct. They were a subsidiary of Polaroid Land. What they did was develop film. They had facilities all over the United States and it was similar to other projects I had been on. Back in the day when cameras had film, you mailed off your film to one of their sites where they developed it and sent back your prints. IBM had contracted to run their IT services. As with almost every other project, most of the people there were previous employees now outsourced. In this case it was to IBM. Basically, they had the same job, but now IBM was getting a cut while signing their paycheck.

The new thing for me was working with a software development team. These were the computer science majors…the real geeks… who were writing the code. They were in the process of putting together an application that was going to be placed in the field at the film-developing facilities. There must have been 20 -30 people all working on one development team.

As I mentioned, I was one exam away from a MCSE and I was an active Microsoft Certified Professional. My responsibility was to build and support the servers and the workstations the new application would run on. I recall thinking how bizarre it was to be at IBM installing Microsoft's operating system on IBM hardware. They were mortal enemies at the time. IBM still had the O/S 2 operating system and I had installed it on my dual boot PC at home. I recall thinking *Why aren't they using O/S 2?*

One of my primary tasks was to keep the work stations in the field locked down so people, or "end losers" as we would call them, could only use the application. Surfing the net was not allowed! Developers would come to me and say, "We want to try this. Can you set us up a work station?" Sometimes I would fly to sites throughout the country and set up servers, load operating systems and fix hardware problems.

It was very insightful to see what is involved in application development and how a team puts it into use. It really pulled a lot of ideas and concepts together I still apply today. I feel fortunate I was able to be a part of that project. I really learned a lot.

As I write I am reminded of a girl I had a fling with while I was there. She was on the development team. She had recently graduated from Clemson as a computer science major and she was very attractive. We worked together and eventually we ended up briefly going out. I had some tattoos from my time in the Corps and have since had many more. At her request, I took her to get the Clemson Tiger paw tattooed on her butt. I thought at the time, and still do; it was just the coolest thing. I am grinning as I write. It was like something out of one of those corny brat pack movies in the 1980's.

Again, the kid who flunked public speaking was now working at IBM and taking a good-looking computer science major to get a tattoo. The shop I took her to was right across the street from NC State campus, near where when I lived as a student. While she was getting inked I reminded her of the night before I played them in lacrosse, me and my buddy went out in town and got wasted. That night we scaled the fence to the football stadium and pissed all over the traditional rock her football team rubs before each home game. Even today when they show their pre-game ritual on TV, I laugh out loud and text my friend. It was all just good collage rivalry banter.

I am reminded of another really good guy I worked alongside while at IBM. He was from Pakistan and his name was Mohammed. Naturally, I called him "Mo," but other times we would call each other "Basha," which I was told meant friend. He would always say, "Ed, come. We discuss." We would share ideas and talk about what we were working on. It is how you learn! Not many people bothered to do this. From my experiences it was very rare. Looking back, when I would figure something out or get some good documentation on a specific problem, my first instinct is to pass it on to help others. It was not uncommon to get a look of "are you nuts?" It's a sad commentary on the corporate world. On the surface everyone preaches collaboration and teamwork, yet the reality is most people are afraid of it.

Once he pulled me aside and said, "Ed? Tell me about this word gonna?" I laughed and explained it to him. He was just a very likable person who I got along with very well. I believe his wife was a doctor studying at Duke. What bothers me to this day is he called and left his number on voice mail, but I could not understand him because of his accent. I really wanted to get a hold of him, especially after 9/11 and what is going on in Pakistan. I was just concerned. I think he was from Lahore. I thought I found him on LinkedIn but it was not him. Maybe someday he will be reading this and he will contact me. That would be nice.

Eventually they brought me on as a permanent employee with IBM. I was no longer a contractor. As I got to know people, the old-timers would tell me what it was like in the past. Some of them had been there when you could only wear the famous white dress shirts. One interesting story they shared was when a byte of RAM was so valuable, departments would spend half their budgets and months fighting over who would get to use it. This is one BYTE or 8 bits of RAM! It is amazing when you consider what is going on today.

The negative I saw at Qualex was that their technology was old. I had been exposed to some of the latest and greatest on previous projects. The word "budget" did not even exist at Glaxo. Developing film was obviously going to become extinct and it did. I had seen newer technologies so I knew what was out there. Cisco and the internet were just exploding on the scene. I was also starting to get tired of having to go up to some director's office because he could not find his Word documents. All this had a bearing when my friend the recruiter called me again.

When I mentioned to my mother I was looking at other positions, she was horrified! Nobody left IBM it was like leaving the mother ship. To some extent, she was right and I had come a long way. I had even framed my IBM offer letter. It weighed on me, but I had done a good job for my friend the recruiter at IBM and I was his go-to guy. Sometimes he would call and ask me to do what we called a "Tech Out." I would speak to potential contractors and ask him or her technical questions based on their resume and then give him my opinion. But now he kept calling asking if would go on an interview for a new position he was trying to fill with 120&20, which had just opened a NOC (Network Operations Center). Once I got in, he had his foot in the door so to speak. I figured the worst they could do is make me an offer, so I eventually agreed.

NOC, NOC, it's the
Corporate body shop

My friend had persuaded me to go on this interview. Naturally, I told him it would cost him, but I really did not believe I would get the job. I had a limited background in WAN (Wide Area Network) support. I had some exposure, but I was primarily a Sys Admin providing operating system, application, hardware and LAN (Local Area Network) maintenance.

120&20 had opened a NOC (Network Operations Center) and was hiring like mad. He told me it would be a sweatshop, but I figured how bad can it be, it was 120&20, a "professional" corporation, right?

I ended up getting the job and in retrospect, I believe it was a typical corporate move of outsourcing regardless of the skill set just to get around the unions. My friend was not kidding; it was bad. It was alleged (wink, wink) contractors were being told to leave after only six months to circumvent the labor laws designation as an employee. (Somehow this was never mentioned to me.) Disgruntled employees were phoning in bomb threats. People were sleeping on the desks because there was no point to even go home; they had to come right back. Older, permanent employees were trying desperately to ride out three more years until retirement. It was like a scene out of the movie "They Shoot Horses Don't They?" (Great movie BTW, nominated for nine Academy Awards.) It really makes my skin crawl how they treated people; calling all permanent employees a "manager" just to get around the unions; that is sophomoric. Every now and then you would hear of someone just standing up and walking out the door. After six months, I was lucky enough to get a position in another department. I hung around until my laptop was stolen by a gang of thieves going around to office buildings. Big, almighty 120&20, with their "body shop" approach, did not have enough sense to get a security guard at night. The only good that came out of there was I had passed a Cisco and a Nortel exam, so I was certified on both platforms to go with my Microsoft Certs. I was so disgusted with the whole place I left; I had, had it!

EDS and President Eisenhower

"Politics is the entertainment division of the Military Industrial Complex." ~ Frank Zappa

By now the oligarchy was beginning to rear its ugly head and taken the once burgeoning dot com industry and fucked it all up, in what came to be known as the "Dot Com Bubble." And thanks to AT&T the local job market was saturated. Despite my skill sets it took nine months before I received a call regarding a contract manager position at a company under EDS, the company started by Ross Perot. Apparently, the Department of the Navy was trying to privatize all the networks throughout the Navy and Marine Corps. This became known as the NMCI project (I for Integration). I spent about a year and half in Virginia at the Little Creek Amphip Base, which is the East Coast home of the SEAL teams. Just being around them was motivating. I would see them running with backpacks and in the gym. I met a few out in town. One of them had hung a lacrosse stick on the wall in a local pub I would frequent and that got us talking. And speaking of pubs this was on a plague left by one of the teams.

Here's to lying,

Stealing,

Cheating,

Fighting,

And drinking.

If you lie... lie for a friend

If you steal...steal a heart

If you cheat...cheat death

If you fight... fight an enemy

And if you drink...drink with me!

I love it! Read it once and never forgot it. Real warriors it was an honor to be in their presence. As for the project, that was another story.

We would show up to a command asking for control of their network so we could integrate it, and they would have no part of it. The same thing happened when I came back to North Carolina to the Marine Corp facility at Air Station Cherry Point. We would show up with orders essentially coming from the Secretary of the Defense. We would ask for an office and phone lines, maybe some chairs and this is how they stoned walled us. They would never provide it or if they did it took forever and it was minimal. It was almost comical because we had eight technicians in one cube sitting on a desk gathered around one phone. Supposedly, there was $7 billion allocated for this project. However, it was the usual textbook inefficiency and waste: all retired military sucking off government contracts. Sometime a retired general would show up for a day, ask what are problems were, promise to take care of it, and then disappear. Another time an individual walked in one morning and announced "I'm here for the asbestos abatement." To which I said "we have not run into any asbestos" and without hesitation he replied "oh you will!" It was really disheartening to see firsthand your tax dollars squandered and abused.

Day after day, nothing was getting done. The worst was at a civilian aircraft rework facility. It was the same one I had delivered helicopters to when I was in the Marines. We would go to meetings and all they would do was inform us of why we could not do something. Excuse after excuse after excuse. What depressed me was they seemed to enjoy it. They would stymie and block us in every way while the 20 project managers over us were screaming to get the work done! For them it was show up and get a paycheck and all I can say is "stereotypes, they come from reality." I recall sitting in a meeting and the onsite project lead walks in and the first thing he says is, "Well, I'm on heart medication now."

This is a picture of Eisenhower's tomb in Abilene, Kansas. I stopped by in my travels chasing work around the country during the great recession. Only an American could come from such a small cow town and rise to such world prominence. He coined the phrase and warned against what he called "The Military Industrial Complex." He also said "history does not long entrust the care of freedom to the weak or the timid."

The icing on the cake was when I received a phone call asking for a reference regarding someone who sort of worked under me...but not really! That gives you an idea of the confusion. As I recall, she was incompetent with no valuable skills. The short of it is despite my personal opinions, I only told the person calling, "She was kicked out of some commands. The commanding officers stated she is not allowed back." That is all I said; it speaks for itself. Ten minutes did not go by and my phone was blowing up. It was a firestorm. I heard shit from other project managers about giving bad reviews, "you can't do that." All I did was speak the "truth" plain and simple. This was another really, bad experience for me. In retrospect, maybe her value was she had a top secret clearance so she gets thrown on government projects to generate billable hours for management. Too bad! I'm trying to get things done; she was inept and obviously had no business being there if for no other reason...she was getting kicked out of commands!

In all we were accomplishing nothing and in my opinion it was borderline criminal how they pocketed your money. It was Eisenhower's "Military Industrial Complex" in all its glory. I ended up leaving pretty much disgusted, and was so embittered I even burned my college diploma. You see for my generation you went to college so you could get to the corporate; that's what we were told. This was my way of symbolically saying it obviously hasn't quite worked out so now I am putting it all behind me.

Off to God's playground, Colorado

While all the EDS crap was going on, I happened to save some money. I was sick of the corporate rat race so I decided to take my brother up on his encouragement to buy land with him in Colorado and start building houses. I saw his video of the huge addition he added to his home, and it sounded like a good idea. I was desperate to get away from the corporate institutions. I thought this was my opportunity. Sounds fantastic, doesn't it? Buy land with your brother and build a house. What a fairytale come true! I have put it on my resume because it sounds great. People say, "You bought land and built a house with your brothers, wow!"

I went there looking to help my brother get established in the building business. I even took a course on General Contracting. Sure I was looking for some financial gain, absolutely; but my thinking was by helping him, I could also help myself. He seemed to have a direction and he had a wife and two kids to support, real estate was as safe as it could get for investing; "They're not making any more land, right!"...how could I go wrong?

Building a home was one of the most arduous things I have ever done. We ended up having to get an extension on the construction loan. It took us 15 months of daunting labor. The house eventually did get completed...well, the top half.

Fortunately, I always kept one foot in the IT world. I ran a small medical clinic's LAN and repaired computers at the ELK's lodge in Telluride. One day when I was at the lodge, someone pointed me out to General Norm Schwarzkopf as an ex-Marine. He lived in Telluride and was there for a pancake breakfast. He was walking out and when he came towards me, without hesitation I snapped right to attention. There is some real truth to the old saying "once a Marine always a Marine" as I had been off active duty for 25 years. As I shook his hand I said, "Sir, it is an honor to meet you." He made a quip about the Marines and went on his way. It was a very proud moment.

My bread and butter was working full-time for a civil engineer who specialized as an expert witness in construction defect litigation. While there I developed an access database, which we used to enter and compile data from onsite inspections. We would extrapolate figures and use it to generate defect reports used as evidence in depositions or in court. I even took an Auto-Cad course at a local community college and passed an exam to become an ICC (International Code Council) home and property inspector. The database was the crowning achievement of my IT career, and without a doubt it was the best job I have ever had.

The house we built and lost

It all came to an abrupt end when his wife left him and he brought his new girlfriend into the office to take my job. I admit that may have been his right, but let me clarify he had only met her maybe a week prior. No wait that's an exaggeration...it was about four days. Thanks to Wall Street, the economy was in free fall and he gives my job away because he is afraid to be alone? So between what I can only surmise as weakness and the oligarchy staging their financial coup d'état of 2008, it was not even close to enough. We lost it all as I had initially feared. After that I installed satellite internet around southwest Colorado, which

I fondly referred to as "God's playground." Often the distances were so great I would sleep in my truck; I was practically homeless.

Chapter 3

Back to the Corporate

The one thing the bad economy could not take away was my accumulation of friends. I have often said, "Bill Gates has got nothing on me." I stay in touch with a lot of people and I had been in contact with an old riding buddy who now lived in Las Vegas. He said, "Come on out, you can move here anytime." When I wasn't traveling for satellite installs, I was staying with my friend in Durango, Colorado. He had found work and was leaving for Texas, so I packed up and headed to Sin City. Viva Las Vegas!

Las Vegas: If you have never been there, I highly recommend it. In fact, like the Hajj or trip to Mecca for Muslims, it should be a requirement of every American to go once in their lifetime; obviously I'm kidding, but if you get the opportunity, go! You do not have to like it, but it is a site to behold.

My buddy was a friend from back East; we used to ride motorcycles together. Now he was a bail recovery agent (aka bounty hunter) and man did he have some stories; apparently bullets bounce off tires!

So there I was set up in a room sleeping on an air mattress, looking for a job. IT (Information Technology) was what I know and it was not long before I ran into a connection. We had an acquaintance we knew from back East and her boyfriend was working in the Clearwire NOC (Network Operations Center). He had worked for Nortel for 20 years building (COs) central offices all over the world until that ship sank. It turned out we had met a few times in a gym in RTP North Carolina, and had some mutual friends. He was kind enough to take my resume. I had one initial interview and within a week I was working.

Imagine sitting at a desk staring at a phone that rings or buzzes incessantly. The only time it does not ring is when you are on the line and the other phones are all ringing in the back ground. The second you hang up, it rings again. This goes on for 12 consecutive hours with the only break coming when you get up and walk outside because you are about to lose your mind. I couldn't take it! I truly believe this would be a violation of the Geneva Convention for treatment of prisoners; it is insane. I ended up staying in the NOC for about 10 months. It pained me; I did not understand what was going on when I talked to the field techs. I wanted to know what they were doing and I could not visualize it. I was always asking them questions. I would say, "I thirst for knowledge." I got to know them well just working together over the phone, and would eventually end up meeting some of them in person.

Because of my interest in field work I applied for positions on-line. Very soon I was contacted by a recruiter. It was a small company for a project doing site surveys in the Minneapolis-St Paul area. Apparently AT&T had bought another cell company and they needed to know what they had purchased. You can't make this stuff up. I wanted to get into the field side of things, so I accepted the offer.

Within days, I was on a flight to Minneapolis, Minnesota. First day on site, I ran into an ex-Clearwire field tech and I recognized his name immediately. We were not on the job for five minutes when he and the other techs all seemed very anxious. Just their demeanor and comments raised my concern. In conversation one of them said Sweden Networks was hiring and I kept it in mind.

Some of them ended up leaving the very next day and it really got me thinking *What have I gotten into?* The account manager came across as very seedy. He would call us "project contractors." Over Christmas the project manager left to go home but would not tell anyone. We all knew he left, but he tried to play it off as if he was still in Minnesota. Just typical under handed management insulting my intelligence bullshit. For me, it was the last straw. I contacted the ex-Clearwire tech whom had left the project on the second day. He gave me the contact information for the SWEDEN recruiter. I'm thinking they are SWEDEN Networks and have been around a hundred years, they have got to be professional, competent, treat their employees with respect, organized; you know a company that has its shit together?

When I called the recruiter, she was very quick to respond. She said to go on-line and look at the position for field techs. I immediately applied for a position in the Southeast using my mother's address in South Carolina. Once it was completed, she said someone would call me for an interview. By the end of the week, I was in negotiations for an hourly rate. She was offering me $18/hour. I said, "But I have a 4-year degree, from a good school." I always throw in "good school." So she countered with an offer of $22/hour and she said, "You get a company vehicle too." So I immediately accepted. Later I would come to regret not getting it in writing.

My desk at the Network Operations Center, NOC, in Las Vegas. I'm surprised management didn't have us sit on anal probes so they could inject even more data and information into us.

I cannot tell you how motivated I was at the thought of being a field tech for SWEDEN working on cellular equipment. I had spent years driving by cell towers and thinking, *How cool would it be to work on those!* And now it might happen.

It was a new lease on life. They were a well-established company and a world leader in the industry. They were the first employer to ever verify I had graduated from college. After all I had been through I was putting the past behind me. I was really psyched! When all of the paperwork was completed, I was instructed to be in Plano, Texas. I was scheduled for three weeks of orientation and training.

I don't know if it was coincidence, but the training in Plano was held in the old Northern Telecom buildings. They looked identical to the ones in North Carolina. The instructors did their best, but openly admitted the training was thrown together, so it was secondary. I was told we were hired because SWEDEN management had let too many field techs go, and they were scrambling to meet the workload. Furthermore, they had a policy once someone was let go; they could not be hired back for two years, not even as a contractor. One of the instructors said he worked for SWEDEN 20 years ago and left to hire on with Northern Telecom. Now they were bankrupt but because he left he was never allowed to come back as an employee.

What concerned me was I had applied for a Southeast position. No one could tell me where I was going. It reminded me of the Marine Corps and waiting for orders. Although this is supposed to be a billion dollar company managed by competent professionals. There was a reason I got of the service? How did they not know where I would be working when they hired me? On the last day of class, I was finally informed I would report to ███████ NC.

When I arrived, I could tell my manager was very surprised. Later, I was told he was informed of my arrival the day before I showed up. Remember, they had been laying people off for the last couple of years. Now a new employee was showing up? It was a very unfriendly environment. Fortunately, I could deal with it. I was older. I work out. I am in good shape, and I am not easily intimidated. Yes, to me it was that unfriendly. That being said, I also make every effort to get along with people.

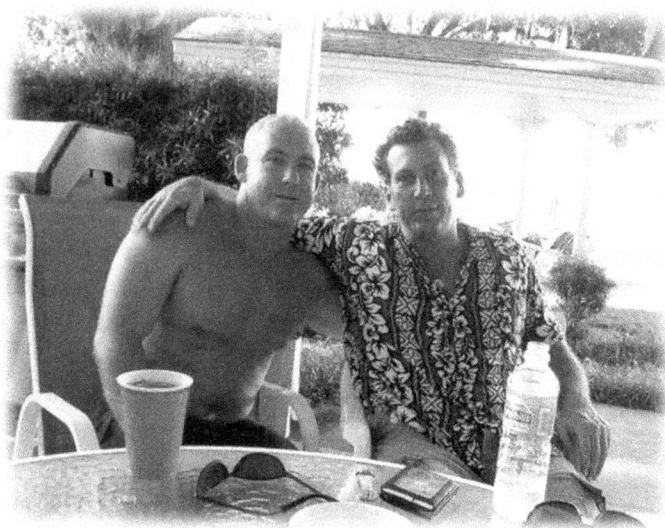

These are two of several good friends who committed suicide on separate occasions; ▮Tommy▮ *(on the left) was software engineer for "Poncho" (wink, wink) Networks. When he would talk about work he would always say "we" because he was loyal and believed it. He told me it was rumored that the porn industry was driving some of their R&D and I had heard that from others in the biz too; it would make sense. It is my belief they basically worked him to death.* ▮Joey▮ *was an ad executive for a local TV affiliate for one of the big networks. When I met him he had a corner office and as anyone in the corporate world knows, that means he was doing well. One of them grew up hand picking tobacco the other started out as a landscaper. No mommy or daddy safety nets here; if these guys threw in the towel something is really twisted with our system. I have lost other good friends to heart attacks and I attribute all of their demise in some capacity to 2008 and Wall St. fucking everyone on the planet.*

The guys I was working with had been together for years. Their pay had been cut and co-workers let go. Now they were making less and working more, which was affecting their family life. Everyone was pissed off and miserable. Now I show up Mr. Sunshine and Lollipops? In reality, I was like a scab. I was hired for less money and brought in to replace people: their friends. Eventually they warmed up to me, but in their defense I understand all of their anger and frustration. I blame management.

As I settled in and started working I would tell people about my job and things that happened at work. Constantly, I got looks of disbelief. People would say, "no way!", "Nobody works those kind of hours" and "aren't there laws against that?"

I decided to keep a diary, which is the centerpiece of this book. It was very much a catharsis for my anger and frustration, which I overtly express in various passages. It is a journal of my "observations" not my "judgments" as that would make me liable. To reiterate my forward as you read, I may come across as a cynic, but think about it this way: *"Maybe the true definition of a cynic is someone who has not yet achieved physical or spiritual atrophy"* (from an unknown author). While you may not agree, I hope you can see where I am coming from, and, if nothing else, you will find some humor: It's in there.

Chapter 4

Give us tools for survival, not weapons

Wednesday, April 27, 2011

I had a ticket for a T-1 installation, which gives a site more bandwidth to better serve you our valued customer. I also I received a T-1 test set from my manager to help with the installation. Problem was the batteries were no good. Fortunately I can use an extension cord because I am close enough to power but if I am in the middle of nowhere its useless. It is a complex piece of test equipment and can be very useful for troubleshooting circuits. This one is beat to shit I can barely read the LCD screen. I also need the User Manual only available on line for $90.00. It will be interesting to see if management allows me to purchase it. Without the User Manual, the test set is next to useless.

This journal entry highlights one of the constant headaches I ran into while working in the cellular industry. The company constantly called on my colleagues and me to perform high tech maintenance and repairs with broken tools and equipment that did not work. The pressure was intense. Management would bombard us with tickets and we were rated on how many we completed and how quickly we finished them. While there was never a problem providing us with plenty of trouble tickets the company was not very good at giving us the "tools" needed to get things done.

Friday May 6, 2011

Email flying around about Roaming and log books.

The argument from my fellow field techs is when they are on site and the customer's network TRACK is down and they have to perform maintenance they have to roam! "How are we supposed to communicate" If the customer's network is down we have to access another available network. It is the cost of doing business. Let me take this a little further. We have been told to stop using the log books at each site because the "the customer does not want to pay for them." Yes the black and white English composition note books that cost about a one dollar will not be provided anymore.

We are all very diligent about log entries because they help when trouble-shooting. We were told to start using one of our applications accessed over the network which if the site is down they have to roam.

In this entry the "tools" are the Log Books and the network. Yes the network, it is a "tool" we need. The problem is to fix the customer's, TRACKs network we must have access to our databases, ticketing applications, site information, trouble shooting applications, IM to the central office techs. All "tools" we NEED...in order to do our job. Here management is telling us not to use it because "we don't want to pay for it."

The kicker is we have been told to stop using the site log books to document maintenance. These are the black and white composition note books that cost a dollar; you have seen them. They have been around so long they have been found in the pyramids. The first lesson in Cellular Field Tech 101: is "on arrival at a cell site check the maintenance log." Often the notes will give you good information on what was done before and help you on where to start to trouble shoot. It's a great "tool" we all use!

Apparently in an executive decision it was decided they do not want to pay for these either. It's been determined it is a "tool" we no longer need; but they can sponsor NASCAR? We have been instructed to only use the "online" application which requires network access? So if we arrive on site and there is no network access…takes us back to the email about "do not roam!" Hello…management? We decided to buy our own note books.

Do you know the story of Archimedes, the ancient Greek mathematician, physicist, engineer, inventor and astronomer? He once famously said, "Give me a place to stand and with a lever I will move the whole world." He calculated with a long enough rod, you could go to a point in outer space, use the moon as a point for leverage, and move the earth. If you worked for the telecomm industry and you got a trouble ticket to realign the earth do to high call drops they would fly you off to that point in outer space without the lever! And then reprimand you for not getting it done.

Monday, May 02, 2011

At last, a day would come that reminded me of why I am writing this journal. When I got into my so-called office (technically I am a remote employee and I do not have an office, but that is another story) my access badge would not work. Maybe they fired me and I did not get the memo?

Eventually a co-worker showed up and let me borrow his badge. After finally getting to my workspace, I booted my laptop and got the BSOD (Blue Screen of Death) TWICE! This consumed another hour. Then I could not enter my time from the Alabama trip because the expense report database was not accepting my codes. To top it all off, my ticketing application where I get my marching orders is still down and I do not know if I am getting tickets assigned to me.

My manager later told me he spent hours on the phone only to find out the group whose sole purpose in life is to support "Facilities Access"... doesn't handle our "facility?" The temp badge I have been using expires every thirty days...not sure what we are going to do?

So here my "tools" are the "badge" for access, the "laptop", the "expense report database", "ticketing application" and the "facilities access group." And none of them work.

I accomplish my job in spite of management's attempts to thwart me. The irony is not lost I work for a company whose business existence is dependent on functioning high tech communications and software. It boggles my mind the high tech "tools" I need do not work accordingly...if at all! The frightening thing is these are not isolated occasions. It happens all the time. I talk to co-workers on the road and it's almost always our main topic of conversation; nothing ever works!

Thursday, May 26, 2011

Holy Shit! Today will be an epic. As always first thing this morning I try to access the internet. This is done through my aircard. It plugs into a USB port and gives me network access via the cellular network. It is a new card that my manger handed me on Tuesday. It worked yesterday because I used it. It is a 4G and 3G aircard and allows you the option to switch between the two. Now when I connect it tells me I have to enter a password? After an hour of trouble shooting just to make sure the problem is not with my laptop I go into the office and tell my manager. He gives me a number to call.

I call and Juan answers, I tell him who I am and what is going on. After about five minutes on hold he sends me to Bill. Same thing, Bill then sends me to Susan who starts to tell me to go to a "web site"? Which I reminded her why I was calling in the first place. Finally her manager gets on and informs me that their group doesn't have access to my account because it is a "special account." I need to contact my account rep. My manger sends out an email for help. Apparently there is a "special" group that supports our air cards. Here is the response:

Dear Ed,

Unfortunately I'll have to have you talk to your super user. I'm thinking its Joe Smith, but I'm not sure. Super users are broken out by director and are listed under the PROGRAM HELP section of the database escalations (if Joe cannot help) then go to Susan A. However, what I believe Joe will tell you to do is call in again for support (thus, getting another person who might know better what is going on). If they cannot help Joe may need to get in touch with THA (Rob Jones) to see if there is a PIN set and if so, how one goes about clearing it.

Here the broken "tool" is my air card. It worked for a few days and then suddenly I was getting login prompts? As you read on it appears the "special group" whose only job is to support the aircard is broken too! And I have never heard of a "superuser" and neither did my manager. The reality is my fellow workers and I figure out how to deal with these situations. Unfortunately we have to fudge things and end up getting creative in ways to work around the roadblocks management continues to throw at us. We have too!

I like to think of it as an American "worker" not a management quality to be innovative when we have a problem to solve. Regrettably the root cause is usually some abstract corporate process originating from some executive leadership team. With regards to the aircard I ended up using the 3G partition which is mind numbingly slow and the latency will kill me especially when I am in the field; but I solder on…

Thursday September 28, 1999 12:30AM

Still have not looked at emails yet, just don't have the time, also I do not have a phone that works. I am waiting for the test phone database…people to activate it? Whoever they are? They just can't hand you a working phone nope! Can't do it! These idiots cannot provide me with a functional tool I need to do my job.

As I read this it makes me wonder if it's some subtle nefarious tactic by management that sets you up for mediocre performance by not having a functioning "phone." That's the only rational idea I come up? Which begs the question why? I can only think it gives them the option to lay you off or be "refreshed" at their discretion for poor performance. Here I spent hours of my own time on a web site trying to get my phone activated here is part of an "automated" response: Automated of course!

> ***From: Test Phone Database***
> ***OU812@testphonehelp]***
> ***Sent: Wednesday, September 07, 1492 3:02 PM***
> *Subject: Action Required - BMW TEST PHONE DATABASE*
> *THA has completed work for transaction #99999. Here is information you may find useful:*
> *Comment: This is not a bulk request as assigned. Please submit under the correct assignment.*
> *Nothing on this request is correct. Request will not be completed under this transaction ID. USMC test*

phone 3170420197 - Not a valid number IMEI
0017010644288890 - Not a valid IMEI
SIM:000826934202330 - Not a valid SIM

*This email message originated
from https://ou812/testphonehelp.com Questions
regarding test phone policies should be directed to
the SSE or super user for your area. A list of
ASSHOLES can be found in the help section of the
program. Technical issues regarding the
APPLICATION ONLY can be addressed to JOE
SMITH JOE>SMITH@ acmetelcomm.com cannot
answer policy questions or assist with
troubleshooting phone issues. Troubleshooting
issues should be directed to the BTSW group by
calling 800-555-5555 on a device other than the one
with an issue.*

*For assistance with this program, it is highly
suggested you log into the program and click on the
HELP link to see if you question is already
answered.*

The **800-555-5555** is the actual contact number posted!
This group is basically saying "we do not know what the fuck
is going on either so we are going to hide behind our web
site." So they're broken too!

Thursday, August 4, 2011 5:50AM

*I had a co-worker accompany me on a calibration last
night. I was surprised since he had been with the company
for years; he was one of the old salts. I had assumed he
would know how to do a calibration blindfolded yet here he
was looking over my shoulder for instruction, that was fine*

with me. It worked out because this site needed two people at night for safety. Every site has a security rating. I don't pay attention to it. Usually I just work alone with my cherry top flashers; I figure if you are really up to no good, you are not going to go towards flashing lights! Plus I have my HK 40. But it really worked out this time that someone accompanied me and it's not why you might think?

Stemming from the animosity of being sold, those left at TRACK have denied me a SWEDEN employee administrative rights on my laptop. They snuck this in on one of the million daily downloads they have automated every time we login. This meant I could not change attributes or enable the network adaptors I needed to perform the calibration. Think of it as removing all the -"W"-'s off the keyboards for the next administration; remember that one? I had to trouble shoot for an hour to figure it out. Fortunately, my co-worker never turned his old laptop in so we used it. It is so demoralizing to have to constantly deal with this internal self imposed bullshit…I just want to do my job!

The "tool" required to do my job was the laptop and if you think about it my own company broke it. The only trouble I encountered that night came from management and their security policies; that policy being "we don't want you to log into the customers cellular equipment to fix it" Good thing there was two of us on site? I reckon a good analogy is going into a fight with one hand tied behind your back. Plus, they don't tell you, you are having the one hand tied until you actually walk into the ring; surprise!

Thursday May 2 2011 6:40 AM

Urgent action required, urgent action required, I must have 15 emails from my manger daily all Urgent Action required and about 25 massages from who knows? One has a power point presentation attachment on how to use some new ordering application. It had 72 slides in it? I have to leave for a site outage.

Speaking of "tools" email! What a wonderful mechanism for communication. Now thanks to the Jack Welsh's of the world it is used to form alliances and craft immunity so you don't get "refreshed" or voted out of the company; and let me digress. Mr. Welsh a renowned corporate leader came up with the euphuism called "refreshing" or the policy of firing a percentage of his work force every year. To me this is not a strategy; this is not even a good idea for one simple reason. Now instead of focusing on the jobs and tasks you are paying people to do you have basically turned your entire work force into contestants in a corporate survival game. No longer is there team work and unit cohesion working to make you money as your fellow employees are now vying against each other more focused on surviving annual layoffs. So if you think about it, instead of running a company he is really more like a game show host.

Just like our ancestors adapted "tools" to deal with their environment, email has evolved into a "weapon" in the corporate survival game. Daily there were so many emails and alerts sent out it would be impossible to keep up with them all. At a minimum, it would take an hour every day to parse your inbox and that does not include replying. Not to mention network latency and connectivity issues like my 3G aircard? The ugly part is most are sent out to cover someone's ass. All titled "Please respond", "Urgent Action Required", "so and so" has requested you click on an Acknowledgement of Receipt. I have been in many a meeting and all you hear is "I sent out an email." If something doesn't get done managers fall back on "Don't you read your emails?" "I sent you an email" knowing you are inundated and can't possibly read them all. I know people who set up a rule in their email app to move selected emails to a folder they created titled "CYA." I don't have to tell you what that stands for? No longer is email only a "tool" for communication it has become a "weapon". It's no coincidence the one app that always works is email?

It's really about functioning "tools" and the acknowledgement of "time" spent implementing their use. Time logging in and reading my email is the same as the time I need on site powering up a test set and analyzing RF spectrums. Both are "tools" I need and the time utilizing them is a reality of business. It astounds me with all their education management fails to comprehend it. Maybe they are too busy sending out their "barrage" of emails...in the hopes of winning immunity. Or maybe they need the help of a union?

Chapter 5

The Company Denies Me Time off by Making Me Waste Time

Tuesday May 10, 2011

I am trying desperately not to become demoralized with all these processes that just mire us down. I received an email from my manager about a missing database item. It basically stated, "YOU" are missing this item. I replied I never received this item. Of course, he replies that I should go to this web portal and order it. Can't just call it a web site? Yet another web site with an ordering application. A co-worker came up to me this morning and said he spent seven hours on the phone with India trouble-shooting his laptop. You can hear the stress in his voice because that is seven hours of lost time that he has no way of accounting for. But it gets better. A new hire recently just showed up at the next market over asking, "How do I get my laptop working?"He drove four hours from Myrtle Beach because he was told there was an IT department there. There is none. It's been outsourced to India. He was turned away and I was told he was almost in tears. I can relate! Here is some of what I deal with daily that I have no why to document: Daily Administrative Tasks not accounted for in the work force software I assume because it doesn't generate revenue…so its conveniently ignored.

> ➤ *Boot up and VPN logins*
> ➤ *Laptop software security patches, application upgrades*
> ➤ *Application trouble-shooting and reloading of vendor software*
> ➤ *Java updates*

- Forced password changes
- Reading Emails
- Company Web casts
- P-card, Travel card reconciliations
- Weekly data correlation and review for SAP and WFM applications along with weekly notes
- Opening trouble tickets within the myriad of incompatible ticketing applications.
- Pulling off the road to IM-txt and correspond with co-workers, calling dispatch and waiting in queue
- On site and travel conditions: snakes, homeless people, prostitutes, hornet nests, vandalism, traffic accidents, road construction, cattle birthing season, bad management.

Ok I snuck "bad management" in there. The one thing you are required to do in the telecom industry is to account for all of your time with in the Work Force Software. Or maybe I should say the Work force software accounts time for you. This is accomplished through what is called a "ticket duration."This includes drive durations calculated by line of site, allotted time spent on repair, calibration work, etc. Actually, let me rephrase that – you have to account for all of your time when the company gives you a code that can then be tied to the accounting department. For anything that cannot be coded the company does not recognize since it does not generate revenue. However, driving to a site as opposed to flying there in your jet pack is a "requirement" and takes time…in order to get it done. This leads to very long, sometimes insane hours especially if you're going to a site out in a pasture and its calf berthing season!

We are being conditioned to sacrifice our all for the company. What does it give the company? More ways to increase its profits. What does it give the worker? You become burned out, tired, achy, and utterly forgotten by your spouse/partner (if he or she stays with you through the nightmare), family, and the dog. But you push on anyway, because everybody knows that working crazy hours is what it takes to prove that you're "passionate" and "productive" and "a team player" — the kind of person who might just have a chance to survive the next round of layoffs.

You could never tell most upper management teams this, but every hour you work over 40 hours a week is making you less effective and productive over both the short and the long haul. And it may sound weird, but it's true: the single easiest, fastest thing your company can do to boost its output and profits -- starting right now, today -- is to get everybody off the 55-hour-a-week treadmill, and back onto a 40-hour footing.

Friday June 24, 2011 11:00PM

I'm sitting on site I happened to check email and I received the following from my manager. It is marked High Importance (every email is high importance?). It read "Attached is a 38 slide power point presentation, on the new vendor application regarding ETS or EOF." I have no idea what ETS or EOF is? So now I will be in the field trouble shooting a site outage with a prescribed time of one hour and I am supposed to go over a 38-slide power point presentation. All while I am being bullied into accepting more tickets

Let's take a short history lesson here on the world of labor. The most essential thing to know about the 40-hour workweek is that, while it was the unions that pushed it, business leaders ultimately went along with it because their own data convinced them this was a solid, hard-nosed business decision.

66

Unions started fighting for the short week in the United States in the early 19th century. By the latter part of the century, it was becoming the norm in an increasing number of industries. And a weird thing happened: over and over -- across many business sectors in many countries -- business owners discovered that when they gave into the union and cut the hours, their businesses became significantly more productive and profitable. How many of us grew up when we had dinner every evening at 6:00 because dad got home around 5:00: better yet remember the dinner bell?

Wednesday May 18, 2011

As we were waiting for the maintenance window, I had a really interesting discussion with my fellow tech last night. He is very good at his job and they would be in a world of shit if he left. To quote him, "I used to get twice as much work done in half the time." We both agreed we like what we do. It is the processes that management continually shoves down our throats that never work as promised that make us want to quit. I told him, "I have always wanted to get a bumper sticker made: You follow process, and I'll get things done!"

I got a call today about a ticket that was going into jeopardy. I told the dispatcher, "I have no idea what that means. Is it from Alex Trebek?" She said, "That's what happens if you don't accept the ticket and if you don't accept it, I have to call your manager." I said, "Why don't you call my mother too?" I accepted the ticket knowing I cannot get to it. I call it virtual harassment.

It blows my mind how management latches on to fads quicker than my teenage niece. I always picture an upper level supervisor reading a magazine and he sees something that increased efficiency at General Motors or Apple. He shares it with the boss and they think it is a great idea to implement that concept in their company. Never mind that this particular company does not make cars, computers, or iPhones! In management's mind, if a process or technique worked in one place, it will work in another.

I was constantly badgered by these situations. Getting the job done took longer and longer. Think for a minute that you wanted to make a peanut butter and jelly sandwich. You take out two slices of bread and the jars of grape jelly and peanut butter. You get a knife and about a minute after deciding you wanted one, you have your finished sandwich.

Now imagine that you undertake the same task, except this time you have to get a "login" for the correct database to order bread and then your manager tells you "the vendor who we have a contract with for jelly only handles strawberry" when you need grape. Then no one can even find peanut butter because it was out sourced. On top of that, you are given a fork instead of a knife to spread the stuff on the one slice of bread because management decided they don't want to pay for two. That sums up many of my days. Oh! And you have 5 minutes or we'll call your mother?

These issues added hours to my day. We had to work long days to begin with. Way too often, incompetence on the part of the company made things that much worse. But as I said, if you bitched or complained you were not a "company man" and you began to feel like you had a target on the back of your shirt. I truly had a desire to be a team player, but I began to understand more and more that I played for a dysfunctional team and what confounded me even more was these are supposed to be educated and smart people? You know damn well they had "leadership" plaques and certificates graduate degrees all over their offices.

When I looked more into where the 40-hour workweek went, I found out that a lot of it had to do with all of the technological development that happened out in the Silicone Valley area of California. People like Bill Gates, Steve Jobs and all of the other techies put in hours and hours of time in developing new software or machines. This became the culture of that particular industry. Of course, when that began to boom, other companies thought that was the blueprint to success.

It did not matter that the software and computer industries were staffed – and I mean this respectfully – by nerds. They were fascinated by this new technology. It became their life and good for them it changed the world without a doubt. But "Everyone can't be the quarterback!" Nor does everyone want to be.

You don't want to live my dream anymore then I want to live yours? To me it's a rather pretentious and arrogant assumption that everyone shares my enthusiasm and wants to make sacrifices usually at the expense of their family for my dream; that's ridiculous and narcissistic. Speaking of, I wonder and from my experiences how many men aspiring to climb or climbing the corporate ladder fail in the basic institution of marriage or family and end up on some sugar daddy web site; it's not that uncommon. For a lot of us, good honest job is a means to an end, not the end itself. Now companies tend to forget the studies showing that working over 40 hours a week actually becomes counter-productive. Management has it ingrained in their brains that they are not doing a great job until they get every last breath out of a worker and demonstrates how corporate America has morphed in to an Oligarchy.

Wednesday July 20, 2011 7:12AM

I am livid! I have spent the last three hours trying to enter codes, codes, and more fucking codes. I have to create an expense report so the company can reimburse me for travel to Alabama.

*One of my receipts for dinner is from the town of Homewood Alabama and it says it right on the receipt! Because Homewood Alabama is not in the database, it will not reconcile that expense. **Error: Required field "City."**And I can't make up a city or put one nearby because it's on the receipt! They'll think I'm trying to scam them or up to something deviant if it all does not match. It is just bullshit! Again, I have to waste my time. I know enough about relational databases. I do not need a dropdown field with every fucking city in the country! Of course, my manager will crawl up my ass to get "your expense reports done."*

I still can't access the CSM (Cell Site Maintenance) app to notify the GNOC (in India) that I will be taking a site down tonight for calibration which means they will be calling the "on-call" when they see the site drop. I would call them myself but I would be waiting "in queue" for 25 minutes to talk to someone who in barely understandable English who will tell me "you need to go to our web site." ...New laptops will be a joy!

If there is ever a chance of bringing real efficiency and decent working hours back to the workplace, it is going to require a wholesale change of attitude on the part of both employees and employers. For employees, the fundamental realization is that an employer who asks for more than eight hours a day or 40 hours a week is stealing something vital and precious from you. Every extra hour at work is going to cost you, big time, in some other critical area of your life. How will you make up the lost time? Will you ditch dinner and grab some fast food? Skip the workout? Miss the kids' game this week? Sleep less? (Sex? What's that?) And how many consecutive days can you keep making that trade-off before you are weakened in some permanent and substantial way? (Probably not as many as you think.) Changing this situation starts with the knowledge that an hour of overtime is a very real, material taking from our long-term well-being — and salaried workers are not even compensated for it and in my not so humble opinion...abused.

So if the company wants me to fight with their apps and processes, it has to be in the context of the eight hour day. When they realize I am spending way too much of my time on their bullshit forms and abstract processes the company may actually have to decide what is really necessary and get rid of everything else.

The original short-work movement in 19th-century Britain demanded "eight for work, eight for sleep, and eight for what we will." Or with an American spin "eight for the pursuit of happiness" and that's your happiness not someone else's. It is still a formula that works.

Wednesday Sept 26, 2012 8:45PM

HR response to my request for YTD (year to date) Over time

As of 9/19/12 Dear   Ed,

Your request   ST0000021349249 , regarding "YTD Overtime" has now been solved.

With the Solution:

Hello Ed,

Thank you for contacting HR

```
Below are the hours of OT you have
logged this year (YTD).

OT Straight - 18 hours

OT 1.5 - 645 hours

2nd Shift OT - 400 hours

3rd Shift OT - 12 hours
```

Do the math!

For employers, the shift will be much harder, because it will require a wholesale change in some of the most basic assumptions of our business culture. Two generations of managers have now come of age believing that a "good manager" is one who can keep those butts in those chairs or trucks for as many hours as possible. With regards to management I believe this approach comes from a confusion in the application of business practices with some historical military conquer. Look! It's "Attila the Accountant, adding his way across the great spread sheets wielding his #2 pencil on his ergonomic office chair ..."general ledger."

A manager who can get the same amount of work out of people in fewer hours is not rewarded for her manifest skill at bringing out the best in people. Rather, she's assumed to be underworking her team, who could clearly do even more if she'd simply demand more hours from them. If the crew is working 40 hours a week, she'll be told to up it to 50. If they're already at 50, management will want to get them in on nights and weekends, and turn it into 60. And if she balks -- knowing that actual productivity will suffer if she complies -- she won't get promoted.

All of this hurts the country, too. For every four Americans working a 50-hour week, every week, there is one American who should have a full-time job, but doesn't. Our rampant unemployment problem would vanish overnight if we simply made an effort to adhere to the labor guidelines.

We will not turn this situation around until we do what our 19th-century ancestors did: confront our bosses, present them with the facts, and make them understand that what they are doing amounts to employee abuse — and that abuse is based on assumptions that are directly costing them untold potential profits. We may have to appeal to the shareholders, whose investments are at serious risk when employees are overworked. (At least one shareholder suit has already been filed against a computer game company that was notorious for working its people 80 hours a week for years on end. It was settled out of court on terms favorable to the plaintiffs.) We may have to get harder-nosed in negotiating with our bosses when we first take the jobs, and get our hours in writing up front -- and then demanding that they stick with the contract down the line. And we also need to lean on our legislators to start enforcing the labor laws on the books. Let me finish with a quote from one of my favorite presidents. *"Knowing what's right doesn't mean much unless you do what's right"* ~ *Theodore Roosevelt*

Addendum: Openly stating "30 years of experience equals nothing" while negotiating pay rates to former employees as you out source them two years before retirement and then try to bring them back as contractors is disrespectful. In fact if we quantify "disrespect" the equivalent metric and dooly warranted reply would be "go fuck yourself" and should be integrated into the subsequent dialogue. Moving operations to a "right to work state" or overseas, so you can circumvent the labor laws while "leveraging" people to work 60-70-80 + hours a week or every weekend knowing they have families and mortgages does not make you a "ruthless" business man. You are NOT a tough guy... and all the money, fancy cars, clothes, big houses; ex-trophy wives, big tips at breastaurants and a V-twin motorcycle will never change that fact. All you are doing is disrespecting the people putting money in your pocket. And this applies to the mistreatment of salaried employees too. Demanding exempt employees (meaning they do not receive overtime) to work constantly insane hours is bullshit! They are professional, that's why you hired them. They will always be available for the "occasional" emergency..."IF!"...you are competent enough to run your company so that every day is not a contest to win immunity.

Chapter 6

Corporate Gobblygook
is its Own Language

S ome corporate gobblygook you may have heard:
Enterprise, Portal, Vehicles, Scalability, The
Cloud, Solutions, Margins, Value Add, Units,
Synergy, Brand, Reverse Mortgage...Venti?

Thursday May 5, 1999

Received this about our bonuses:

Team,

*In our all-hands meeting, I announced our S Term
Variable (STD) objectives and weightings, but I wanted
to provide you with more details on the program. The
specific objectives for each employee group are listed
below, but basically, all of us will be measured on
operational performance – how well we deliver for our
customers -- and financial performance.*

*Half of our objectives focus on operational excellence
and customer satisfaction. The other half focuses on
OU812 overall financial performance and contract-
specific financial performance:*

*•AFU Weighted Capital/Net Sales: Measures progress
on AFU overall financial targets (annual)*

•MS Contract Margin: Measures how well we are doing financially on a particular contract or group of contracts (semi-annual)

•Customer Service Level Agreements: Measures operational performance – how well we are delivering on our contracts (semi-annual)

•OU812-AFU and Project Customer Evaluation Indexes: Measures the results of customer surveys (annual)

•OU812 Motivation Index: Measures employee motivation, based on Dialog results (annual)

The weightings reflect whether you're more involved in Managed Services or Support ACME business overall. As a result of our integration into ACME Inc., former ESI will align this year with the standard OU812 STD plan. This alignment with the OU812 plan may change your current STD Commitment Level – which is your target bonus incentive based on a percentage of salary.

Your manager will discuss any 1935 STD Commitment Level changes with you in the next few weeks.

The quality of our execution will determine our success. Even as we face constant change, it's imperative that we keep our focus on delivering with excellence for our customers. Let me take this opportunity to thank you for your hard work and all you do to please our customers.

A Motivation Index are you kidding me, based on "Dialog" and what exactly is Operational Excellence or Quality of Execution...better yet "delivering with excellence"? Is that compared to a "delivering with mediocrity?" Don't get me wrong I am grateful for a bonus, but! I can speak for all of us, we would rather have them keep it and hire more techs. Some time off now that would be a bonus! I am sure they have it calculated they made far more money by throwing us a small bonus then hiring more techs…fuckers!

One day I was in my manager's office and I asked him a question. I do not recall the specifics because he looked at me with this ridiculous expression and replied *"we have vehicles for that."* I just felt insulted because he was not talking about wheels and an engine. It was an absurd response and he knew it.

All industries have their own language and telecom is no different. However, I think they specifically pay someone just to create buzzwords and acronyms to make the business seem mysterious and elitist. What it really does is make everything damn confusing to their employees and the public and to me it smacks of deception.

The only reason the company I work for is in existence is because of communication. Most problems in this world, including those in the business, usually result from the inability of people to talk and listen to each other. Take a relationship between two people, international tension among countries, or an employee trying to understand what a boss wants, and it all comes down to an inability to communicate. I reflected many times that communications in my *communication company* sucks!

It does not help when you are not speaking the same language. Oh, it is in English, but you should not have to reach for a business-speak to English dictionary to translate what the higher ups want the employees to know. It reminds me so much of when I have had to deal with legal documents in my life. A simple lease or documents to purchase a house can have you reach for the Excedrin as you are trying to wade through all of the legalese that mucks up the English language. I often think that those documents would boil down to a couple of paragraphs if you got rid of all the bullshit. Of course, I believe lawyers write that way on purpose...so you have to keep hiring lawyers! Personally I find it arrogant and disrespectful.

By the same token, I have to wonder why corporate America goes out of its way to make their communications so laden with jargon. It seems to me that if they want to direct their employees to do things in a certain way, it would be well worth their time to communicate that in a clear, concise way. I have enough to do just figuring out all of the technical equipment I use and the codes to put in my reports to do my job correctly. When I get my umpteenth "Extremely Urgent" memo, and then my eyes glaze over trying to decipher it, where does that get any of us?

I wonder if at executive staff meetings or corporate board rooms, do the bigwigs sagely nod as they read and listen to reports but inside are saying, "What the hell are they talking about? I will have to get back to my office later and figure all of this out!"

I am a team player and believe that what I am doing is important for my company. But it is incredibly frustrating when I am not sure what they are trying to say. What is wrong with using plain, simple language and not trying to impress everyone with the hot business buzzword or phrase of the day? Believe me, you are not impressing those of us in the trenches who make your company operate. You just make it more difficult to figure out what the hell we are supposed to be doing or what you are trying to convey.

This type of "communication" is not restricted to the executive halls of power. Check out this next entry that shows the same problem exists on the grassroots level of operations:

Friday June 24, 1999 11:00PM

Verbiage from one of the daily bulletins:

> *The OBGY is moving to a regional reporting structure on 01/31/1776. There will be 75 OBGY Managers; one per region. The Technicians are moving from a national to regional model so we can realize greater synergies by softening the line between VSO and PSO Technicians while assisting each other with work load. The PSO will remain in their current local environment and VSO will report to a physical location to meet business needs. The transition will build a solid foundation for productivity and efficiency while maintaining uninterrupted work flow.*

When I get stuff like this, it drives home exactly why I am keeping this journal. Write on!

The people who come up with this shit are patting themselves on the back about how they are making things better. We just want to cry! This was in reference to our shortage of Central Office techs THAT'S IT! All they did was slide what regions of the country they serviced while other techs came into the office instead of working from home. We/they are still woefully under manned absolutely nothing has changed, NOTHING!

What is evident to me with what I have put up with is that communication in this fashion only flows one way – downhill. If you really want to make something work better, it seems to me that the people trying to improve a company process would want to talk to the technicians who have to do the actual work and then call things what they are. That rarely happens in this business, if at all; can you say "Union?" I know there are companies where communication consistently flows throughout the company. I guess these are the enlightened businesses that want to optimize their profits over long term operations, because they go hand-in-hand.

Here is another excerpt from my journal where I felt like a 10lb sack of assholes in a 5lb bag. In other words, a really bad day:

Friday August 5, 1999 7:20AM

Check this out, I came across it while I was trying to find instructions on getting applications I "NEED" to install on my new laptop. (apps) just like you download and install to your smart phone. (SAME CONCEPT) This will cure insomnia!

To add a new customer, a Request For Service should be raised by the local Market Unit and sent to the e-mail address MDSP CR (EAB) with a PO for the analysis enclosed. All Requests for Service that do not follow the template available in above link will be rejected. To order an MSDP account, Oracle access or access to NIM Light, please follow the instructions for Central User Provisioning (CUP) below. For access to other ACME Tools, please follow the described process on the IT Support page to submit a Service Request. Central User Provisioning (CUP) Central User Provisioning (CUP) system is a self-service access management tool, handling access to the various MSDP Oracle client application environments and to the ACME Tool NIM Light. Access is requested through a Self Service web page. Please note that for the centralized tools such as ACME Resolution/OneTM, TeMIP, Business Objects etc. you also have to submit a Service Request to order an account to the specific tool. The Central User Provisioning is a generic process to be followed by all ACME users. The local processes for access management within each NOC are determined internally, and do not need to be altered as a result of CUP.

Important note: The current implementation of CUP excludes the user base located at NOC Reading since the Reach Transformation Program is ongoing. This means that all user accesses for NOC Reading should be managed via Service Requests.

Did you make it this far? Talk about "gobblygook", I went to college. I am reasonably intelligent. I just need applications to load on my laptop SO I CAN DO MY FUCKING JOB! Just like you put on your cell phone. Not launch the space shuttle? When you read something like this and go "huh?" something is really wrong. This was a little worse than an average day, but it is more typical than I care to admit.

Thursday September 28, 1999 12:30AM

Email from manager regarding new weekend rotations

Subject: RE: New weekend rotation:

The plan will be to change it so that you work Wed-Friday on your on-call week and then Wed-Friday the week after. This way during your on-call week, you will probably work Mon-Tuesday night with On-Call issues and Wed-Sunday as your regular work week.

The next week, you would have Monday and Tuesday off unless we need you to come in. Then work Wednesday through Sunday. The next week you would work Mon-Fri. In this scenario, the most you would work consecutively is 10 days in a row. (a 4 day improvement) Sounds good?

Yippee! We only work 10 ten days in row which is bull shit. But no clear definition of "on-call" specifically in the "work force software" so I requested clarification:

> Jorge,
>
> Can we get some clarification or description of what the responsibility is for "on-call" designation in WFS? It appears to be very vague and ambiguous, also wondering On-Call is performing scheduled maintenance?

Reply from manager explaining: "On-Call"

> Ed
>
> On-Call is when you are on "Stand By" to work tickets that are Priority 3 or higher. In an effort to reduce OT, the Pri 3's can be done in the morning if they are late enough in the day/evening that they do not violate the SLA. With that said, you have to be sure that the ticket is assigned to you for your first ticket in the morning. If you have a carrier add or T1 Augment already assigned to you as your first ticket, then we should still be able to run the previous nights ticket. (Unless the ticket is too far away from where your carrier add or T1 augment is. At that point in time, you will give me a call and we will work it out.

The above entry can also go under the chapter titled: "You can't make this stuff up."

"Never tell people how to do things. Tell them what to do and they will surprise you with their ingenuity." - George S. Patton

Chapter 7

A Little Common Sense Would Go a Long Way

Wednesday May 11, 2011

No equipment upgrades last night due to weather. Started off this morning with a ticket for a bad I/O card that I had recently replaced. What happens is the initial ticket cannot be completed or "resolved" until the transaction of the parts takes place in the inventory databases. While in the middle of this task, my laptop crashes or blue screens so I lose another twenty minutes rebooting.

Then I receive a ticket for a high temperature alarm in a neighboring market. I called dispatch and said, "It will be a good hour or more before I can get there. Are you sure this ticket goes to me?" She says, "You are the only tech nearby." I said, "No problem."

The site was very difficult to find. I could see the tower off in the distance; I just could not find the access road because there were so many. I had to keep trying one at a time driving into someone's drive way only to turn around. When I did find it, it was next to a Big Cat reserve. I drove right by a cage of lions which was pretty wild. (Get it?)

When I opened the shelter door, I was blasted by the heat. Obviously, the HVAC was not functioning. What worried me was the battery strings cooking off while I was inside; it happens. First, I reset the circuit breakers to the

HVAC. This did not work and I did not think it would, but I had to try. I decided to shut down some non-essential equipment and leave the door open. I'm only in there for a minute, basically holding my breath. Between the fumes and the heat that is about all one can take.

I called my manager to let him know, and he said to send an email to the GNOC (Global Network Operations Center) and the market manager. Bring up the equipment you took down and close it all up. This really bothered me. I asked if I could at least keep the door opened. We were in a fenced compound in the middle of nowhere. He said, "No!" I will bet all the equipment will be cooked. It is summer in the south. I find it ridiculous that they do not have a HVAC on call.

On the way back, I got an email from my manager about my DR coding (Alabama Disaster Recovery expenses). I replied, "Use the XYZ application right?" he shoots back, "No! Use ABC application for DR." I should have known?

The Wikipedia definition for **Common Sense** is that it is a basic ability to perceive, understand, and judge things, which is shared by ("common to") nearly all people, and can be reasonably expected of nearly all people without any need for debate.

This concept seems to be greatly lost in corporate America in general, and the telecom industry as a whole. Look at a very simple concept inherent in the journal entry above. My entire job deals with technical equipment, computers, etc. One of the basic aspects of all of this equipment is that they put out heat. The time I talk about here was spent in North Carolina, a state that feels somewhere between a steam bath and an oven in the summer. "It's not humidity its heat and stupidity" is what we would say.

It was incredible to me where so much hinged on having temperatures in these buildings kept to a level where everything functioned properly, that the telecom giant I worked for did not think enough to keep a HVAC tech on the payroll. With benefits, you figure a guy like that would cost all of $100,000 a year or so. How much more money would be saved if you had someone like that going out and servicing the air conditioning systems on a regular basis as well as being available to troubleshoot problems when they popped up?

This is only one occasion where, from my point of view, the management hierarchy misses the obvious. I do not know if vision is clearer when you are down in the trenches, but it often seemed like simplifying many corporate procedures and having qualified employees on staff would have made all of us much more efficient and provided you with better service.

I learned long ago that a corporation should always try to be making a profit; I get it. I just thought a little common sense would go a long way to making that happen. The HVAC problem was only one of many things I put up with that had me shaking my head in disbelief. Here is another:

Thursday, May 26, 2011

Myself and another tech requested we get certified to climb the towers. Sometimes connections and antennas go bad or microwave links need to be realigned, lighting strikes, birds, wear and tear by the elements. Other climbers step on connections. The new LTE equipment that is being rolled out has the radios mounted behind the antennas on the tower and it is not uncommon for them to go bad. This was another reason we pushed to get certified to climb. When I asked my manager in person he mumbles "well…I'm not sure" and of course won't look me in the eye...I just keep thinking what a bunch of fucking idiots?

It all means your calls dropping and it will state right in the ticket: "site is experiencing high call drops, please investigate." When a site has high drops we hook up a test set and check for reflective power measured in decibels (db) running up and out the antennas. If we determine the problem is up the tower then someone needs to repair it. The climb course is a week and I even told my manager if he pays for the course Ill supply my own climbing gear.

The SOP is to call for a tower crew which takes days if not weeks. Sometimes the repair never gets done because management does not want to pay for it as it can cost thousands of dollars. They decide it's cheaper to just let your calls drop. Here you have two techs that want to climb. We could be sent to neighboring markets too. Two of us have made the request several times and it gets ignored. Think of the money that would be saved and they won't do it? It defies logic...mean while your calls drop like anchors.

I think it is easier to get Congress to accomplish something...and we all know how difficult that is! Sometimes the bureaucracy I have to go through makes me feel like I am in the middle of Abbott and Costello's *Who's On First?* I have to tell you that there are many times my laptop almost went flying out of my truck's window. Between the shitty equipment I was issued, and the labyrinth of passwords and websites we had to navigate and managements grasp of the obvious it is a marvel that I got anything done?

I do not know at what level in a company's chain of command they lose the ability to deal with matters on a practical scale aka reality. I reckon us grassroots people look at what we need to do on a pragmatic level. We are given all of these procedures and checklists, but when push comes to shove, we will use our ingenuity and experience to do whatever to get the job done. I started talking about the HVAC issue at the beginning of this chapter. Here is a later entry that put further light on how screwed up things were.

Thursday July 14, 2011 5:40AM

First ticket was an over temp alarm at a site in Charlotte, I was at this two nights ago. It is about an hour and fifteen minute ride. Well, I see high temp and I jump right on it because it is the summer and if the HVAC goes, we have real problems. After an hour and half drive I get to the site and everything is fine. AC is running so who knows what this was all about? All part of this automatic ticketing system, I guess?

Next ticket was for an alarm that I checked and did not see it (the alarm) in the support app. Common sense would say close the ticket, but I cannot just start clearing tickets early because it is automated and I have to cover my time for each ticket. If I close out all my tickets to soon then it looks like I am sitting on my ass. It is insanity! Therefore, the system sees me in progress working on one site while in reality I am working on high temp alarm at another site. When I arrive, I can feel the heat coming off the door so I know it is legit.

Here is the process to get HVAC repaired. See if you can follow? I have to go through the initial opened ticket for high temp alarm. But before that, open another app where you report HVAC outages, in that application I have to go through the "request a login." This emails me a link, which takes me to a setup your password profile, which makes me go through three Captchas because my password was not secure enough. Meanwhile, we have a site literally burning up. I opened a ticket for an HVAC repair as critical. Only then can I take that ticket, go back, and enter it into the original ticket which gets closed yes "closed" as...ready for this? "Unresolved" We close tickets as unresolved? I left the shelter door open. It is in a fenced and secured compound and I don't care.

Talk about closing the gate after all the horses ran out and they want SLA's! I am spending all my time trying to let the company know that they need to do something to get a building cooled down and that all of the components are being fried. I am sure if a few of their buildings went up in flames and they lost millions of dollars in equipment and customer grumbling, then the company may start thinking about handling the HVAC issue in a different way. On second thought...NA! They would not change a thing! I guess what separates the good companies from the bad are that the good ones figure out what they need to do and implement it **before** something burns to the ground; probably with the input and help from the unionized employees?

Saturday September 3, 2011 8:20AM

Dispatched again, I called the GNOC twice to verify if this site is down they said yes, it s a fuckin long drive, this should be a Charlotte tech its right on the edge of the market, this just fucking sucks! Still a good hour and half if not more. I looked at one app, its telling me we lost the site about 5AM but I also see alarms coming in after that, so I don't know, I see later alarms, who knows? It says in the ticket with a name they called and commercial power was verified by the power company. If I get there and the site is down because of no power I will go ape shit! I dread this drive...

***3:20PM** GUESS WHAT! I pull up on site and its eerily quiet, and that means one thing, NO COMMERCIAL POWER!, WTF! So that's what I put that in the ticket in all* caps with a bunch of exclamation points. *Except the "W.T.F"... I called dispatch and asked "who put COMM power was verified in the ticket?" she said "the GNOC" AAAH! REALLY!...*

Plain and simple if commercial power was verified down I would not have had to drive to the site and the company would not have wasted thousands of dollars. In some cultures when people in positions of power really fuck things up for the many they have the decency and honor to go outside and "fall on a sword" Not here! Whoever moved the "NOC" (The idiots that verified commercial power in the ticket) to India probably got a raise and promoted to an executive leadership team? To me it is a good example of how the executive elites are becoming even more disconnected and turning us into a two class society.

Where I worked could have been so much more productive without all of the nonsense that management foisted on us. And that nonsense was born out a "well my data told me to do it." A detachment that was inherent in all their decisions and by ignoring "realistic" ideas coming from us the workers. In the end they have alienated the very employees and customers that are going to make them money. It doesn't have to be this complex there are companies out there that are successful with a simpler approach and it's even documented. Similar to the title of this chapter Robert Fulghum published a *New York Times* bestseller that sums it up. *All I Really Need to Know I Learned in Kindergarten.*

Chapter 8

Management Tends Not to Care About Employees as People

Sunday April 8, 2012 6:20PM

It's Easter Sunday and I have all ready worked 10 hours today. I stopped by my mother's house to get a home cooked meal (a real treat for me... pun intended) and to see my brother. I just received a text from my manger it read; "Are you going to work more tickets?" I texted back "No! I can't, its Easter Sunday and I just found god." I thought that was funny. I didn't get a reply. Fuck him!

The only thought that comes to mind here is now you have disrespected me and my family and I almost consider this to be an invasion of privacy. If maintaining the network is so critical, so dire, if you really care so much about the customer then...HIRE MORE FUCKING PEOPLE!

Friday, June 3, 2011

I wrestled with our new RMA,(Return Material Authorization) application. I took a drive test with a generator in tow, had to back it up and turn it around. Not sure what kind of certification this is. It is not a CDL.

There was all hands mandatory meeting at 8AM under the guise of a vehicle inspection. I was going to go but I basically said fuck it they can check my vehicle at the

90

*beginning of my shift. Come to find out it was not an announcement, they let people go. Not anyone in our market but the next market over. How ironic I received a call from dispatch this afternoon about some priority-3 tickets in jeopardy. I said I will take them and asked where? She said "Charlotte." It's three and half hours away in the market that just lost FT's, **management brilliance!** I couldn't go its far.*

Monday April 4, 2011

I spoke to woman in dispatch who has been working there for 25 years. I asked her sarcastically if they gave her a watch on her anniversary. She said they sent her a crystal glass with etching. I said, "Oh, a chunk of glass." She said, "I was pretty disappointed that no one gave it to me in person; someone just left on my desk." "I think she said she threw it out.

My manager keeps ignoring my requests to expense the purchase of the User Manual for my T-1 test set. I am tempted to just pay for it myself.

I have two thoughts as I look back over this entry and they are actually related. It has to do with management's attitude towards the people they are supposed to be supervising. Look at the T-1 test set I talked about. This is a great piece of equipment that can improve efficiency when working on T-1 lines and cut down on the time, and thus the cost, of working on them. Now, does anyone else think it is ridiculous that I am looking for a User's Manual online and worrying about if my company is going to be paying for it or not? I am an employee of this telecom giant that makes millions on millions and they do not have enough regard to give me the tools *and* the information I need to use them correctly.

An employee is supposed to receive all of that stuff from the company that employs him. Unfortunately, when employees are only looked at for how much work they accomplish and how many tickets are closed, it seems like management forgets they are people. By its very definition, management is the function that coordinates the efforts of people to accomplish goals and objectives using available assets efficiently and effectively. If managers are only concerned about meeting goals and numbers and forget that the other part of their job is making sure the people have the required tools, then the results are going to be less than ideal. A manager has to *work* with the people who report to them. Not just treat them as data in spread sheets and mouse clicks in a work force application.

This shines through regarding my second thought from this entry. The woman who received her award for 25 years said she was, "disappointed that no one gave it to me in person." Would it kill somebody in upper management to take the five minutes to bring the recognition to this lady in person? I'm willing to bet no one in upper management even knows about her. This is why so many line employees look at management as arrogant assholes.

Sunday January 22, 2012 6:40PM

My manager approached me and asked me if I had home internet. It kind of caught me by surprise but without hesitation I said "no! Why would I? I am never home... cause I'm always working" He mumbled something; the insinuation was I should have it. I guess I sounded a little sarcastic about the never being home, but it was true! And I thought it was even a little humorous. Then I said "I just use my aircard" And added "you designated us remote employees... if you pay for it I'll get it" knowing that would never happen.

In his world I'm supposed to have home internet that I pay for out of my pocket to use for work. And for the record every company I have ever worked for allowed you to expense your internet if they required it. And if they didn't pay for all of it they paid for most of it and to me even that's fair. But here If you really think about it I work for two of some of the largest telecommunications and networking corporations in the entire world! ...And they want me to provide them with internet service... WOW!

Friday, May 13, 2011

Interesting discussion with my manager. It came up about traveling to other markets to help out. I immediately volunteered and this somehow leads to talking about budgeting and hiring. He said, "Our director wanted to slide people around rather then fill positions only to let someone go later." "How about that for forward thinking!" I said. "That's really cool!" He said, "Yeah, some directors just want bodies and then when the project is over they don't care – goodbye."

Somehow, I missed a call and when I checked my messages, it was someone asking me the status of a ticket. It was not the GNOC, and it was not the dispatch but some other group? I reluctantly called back and asked in an agitated tone, "What group are you with and what is your function?" He said his job was to monitor tickets and SLA's (Service Level Agreements). I wanted to say "why don't you get off your ass and come help us in the field?" I take it as an insult. Why would I not do everything as fast as I passably could? To me the sooner I finish a job, the sooner I can forget about it. It is called a "sense of urgency." I alluded to this and said, "How can I get anything done when I have to stop and constantly update people?" He said, "Well, I can expedite things and I have direct contact with vendors." I

93

tried to be polite and said, "I will keep your number." I can tell you if he starts calling when I am working I will not answer. It is harassment!

There is no doubt in my mind that a company's culture dictates a lot of the attitude throughout the corporation. I think for every one of us in the field there was twenty people sitting at a desk. It seems to be a prevailing attitude today, part of this "I am educated with a college degree" so now I'm better than everyone... who does "work". Never mind the degree was bought "on-line" but has anyone bothered to look at a calendar; that attitude is just plain tyranny.

If the people at the top have the cannon fodder mentality; that will be the management way of doing things throughout the place. Maybe this works for the stockholders for a short time, but it is not a recipe for long-term success. A good indication of this self-destructive management style is to look at employee turnover including contractors. If human resources have a revolving door that looks like it is powered by a steam turbine, then that company may need to do a reality check on how it manages its personnel. Again I can only think of the unions as way to address this problem.

You can also see from this journal excerpt the extremes I worked concerning management styles. The beginning of my shift I talked to someone who seemed to have a good handle on how to work with people, and who had a sense of what would be good for the company and the employees. A short while later I get harassed by a new layer of management whose sole purpose seems to be that of hall monitor in a grammar school.

Me and most of my mates looked at ourselves as professionals. If someone wasn't getting work done it would not take long to figure out. But everyone works differently and every situation is unique. It was ingrained in us to do our job as well as we could and as quickly as possible. We all went through a hiring process? That is what is meant by being a professional. It does not mean having some internal affairs department looking over our shoulders in addition to all the other layers of management. All it really does is slow down the repair process.

Saturday June 12, 2011

I received a ticket for an outage and I believe this was an auto-generated ticket as opposed to being sent through dispatch. The notes in the ticket said T-1 unreachable. I called the GNOC support number and listened to the 25 prompts until I heard circuit testing. I was hoping it would take me to "on-call" Tier II, which was someone that could check in some application and see if the site was up. This would save me an hour drive to the site. After following the prompts, I ended up back with Dispatch who stated, "I guess no one is working because it's the weekend." I said, "Yeah, I guess you're right. Must be nice" so I drove out to the site.

Upon arrival, everything looked OK as I figured it would. I checked the circuits and all the equipment was up. While I was there, I received a ticket for a site I was at yesterday. I called into dispatch and said I am near the Virginia border and there is no way I can get to that site. I asked why the local market "on-call" could not handle it and she said, "He was blocked out." That meant his manager had blocked the "on-call" in the work force software. I said very sarcastically, "That's interesting? Being on call but not really being on call; how does that work?" She said, "He must be tired or had worked long hours." I said, "Welcome to my world." While I was on the phone, another ticket came in for the same market. I said, "Another ticket just came in. I cannot get to them. I am two and half hours away."

She said to just make something up and she would move them out to next week. Remember, it is all about the SLA's (Service Level Agreements) and that is what makes this all so pressing. I put notes in both the tickets "No Site Access" as the reason I did not work it. Just made up bullshit for the SLA's we'll see what happens Monday. If my manager asks me what the site access issue was, I am going to say, "Excessive distance between me and the site entrance door."

I do have to say that it was nice for a manager to give the "on-call" guy a break if he was exhausted. I can count on the fingers of one hand how many times that happened to me when I had that designation – none! Looking back on this situation, and without the sarcasm I had at the time, it was a good thing. I know from experience that you become worthless in this job if you reach a state of complete burn out.

Often, all I was to management was a truck who did their bidding. The fact that my colleagues and I were very real people who worked hard didn't not even matter; we were no different than some Slavic immigrant working in the steel mills at the turn of the last century. They figured they paid us, so they owned us and that is all there was too it.

We all work for a paycheck, but smart managers realize that getting good performances from the staff under them takes more than a paycheck. There was a work experiment done years ago. It was in the manufacturing arena, but the lessons hold for any management/employee scenario.

In this experiment, the manufacturing team was split up in two groups. The first group was paid more money and got to work in an environment that was brightly lit and had all the latest machinery. They were told to go to work and were pretty much left alone by supervisors, except when it was necessary for someone to come in and yell at them.

The second group had a dingy cramped area to work in with machinery on its last legs. They were getting the same wages they always did. The difference here is that managers were always present. However, their job was to encourage and to work with their employees. Workers were recognized for a good job, and managers were looked on as a very positive influence and it was a real "team" effort in getting the work done well.

This second group is the one who performed best out of the two. They left the ones behind in the dust who were making more money and had the better working conditions. You see, management can make a huge difference in business. When they remember that they are working with people, and to treat people with respect and encourage them be successful in their tasks, then everybody flourishes. Sadly this type of management style has disappeared and I believe its extinction is another "unintended consequence" of the information or digital age.

Chapter 9

A Call to Union

Monday May 23, 2011

The myriad of emails have started flying. As usual can't even begin to read them there are so many and being Monday it's even worse. I finally said screw it I can't sit here and fuck around with all these logins and data entry bullshit I have work to do and took off for another PM (Preventive Maintenance). I always feel better when I can accomplish something tangible. On the way I had to pull over and IM dispatch. IM is the preferred method to communicate; of course they make us sign an affidavit that we won't IM or eat and drive. If we call in through we have to wait in queue for 15 minutes so we IM and drive we have to! Hell if I didn't I would never get out of the driveway. Dispatch is woefully under manned. I pulled over this time because I got into a lengthy conversation and it was just ridiculous trying to keep driving. I still need to perform a vehicle inspection that is past due. So now, I am a mechanic and DOT inspector on top of being a cellular field tech. It amazes me how they indiscriminately dump tasks on you then refuse to acknowledge the time it takes. That is why we need to unionize.

I saw snake skins in the shelter where I did the PM. You always have to be careful especially in the summer. I will have to ask my manager if the work force software has a code for "snakes" or "waiting in queue" when you call dispatch.

Unions have become a big, bad word in America. They are seen as the culprit that brought America to its knees. It is said that unions are responsible for inefficiency in the workplace, lazy workers, and expensive products. If you look at all of the material that demonizes unions, you will discover they are also responsible for acid reflux and the demise of the little rascals.

They say history is written by the victors. That is so true of how labor unions are looked at now. Since they are in decline and are treated as a form of the Ebola virus, most of the revisionist history concerning unions is misguided. It was unions that helped transform America into a powerhouse where owners, management, and employees shared in the wealth; hence a "middle class." So if unions are so bad, why does our current economic landscape in the United States continue to be a widening gulf of the *have's* and the *have-not's*?

Let's have another history lesson here. The roots of our country's trade unions extend deep into the early history of America. Several of the Pilgrims arriving at Plymouth Rock in 1620 were working craftsmen. Captain John Smith, who led the ill-fated settlement in 1607 on Virginia's James River, pleaded with his sponsors in London to send him more craftsmen and working people.

Primitive unions, or guilds, of carpenters and rope makers, cabinetmakers and cobblers made their appearance, often temporary, in various cities along the Atlantic seaboard of colonial America. Workers played a significant role in the struggle for independence; carpenters disguised as Mohawk Indians were the "host" group at the Boston Tea Party in 1773. The Continental Congress met in

Carpenters Hall in Philadelphia where the Declaration of Independence was signed in 1776. In "pursuit of happiness" through shorter hours and higher pay, printers were the first to go on strike, in New York in 1794; cabinetmakers struck in 1796; carpenters in Philadelphia in 1797; rope makers in 1799. In the early years of the 19th century, recorded efforts by unions to improve the workers' conditions through either negotiation or strike action became more frequent.

By the 1820s, various unions involved in the effort to reduce the working day from 12 to 10 hours began to show interest in the idea of federation; that is the joining together in pursuit of common objectives for working people.

As ineffective as these first efforts to organize may have been, they reflected the need of working people for economic and legal protection from exploiting employers. The invention of the steam engine and the growing use of waterpower to operate machinery were developing a trend toward a factory system not much different from that in England that produced misery and slums for decades. Starting in the 1830s and accelerating rapidly during the Civil War, the factory system accounted for an ever-growing share of American production. It also produced great wealth for a few, and grinding poverty for many.

With workers recognizing the power of their employers, the number of local union organizations increased steadily during the mid-19th century. In a number of cities, unions in various trades came together in citywide federations. The Nation Labor Union, an organization of local unions formed in 1866. The NLU eventually persuaded Congress to pass an eight-hour day for Federal workers. Never very strong, it was a casualty of the sweeping economic depression of 1873.

The next big step was when Samuel Gompers founded the American Federation of Labor in 1886. Gompers, born in 1850, came as a boy with his parents to America from the Jewish slums of London. He entered the cigar-making trade and received much of his education as a "reader" (a worker who read books, newspaper stories, poetry and magazine articles to fellow employees to help break the monotony of their work in the shop) and became a leader of his local union and of the national Cigar Makers Union.

A statement by the founders of the AFL expressed their belief in the need for more effective union organization. "The various trades have been affected by the introduction of machinery, the subdivision of labor, the use of women's and children's labor, and the lack of an apprentice system so that the skilled trades were rapidly sinking to the level of pauper labor," the AFL declared. "To protect the skilled labor of America from being reduced to beggary and to sustain the standard of American workmanship and skill, the trades unions of America have been established." Thus, the AFL was a federation that organized only unions of skilled workers.

In 1911, a fire broke out at the Triangle Shirtwaist Co. on New York's lower East Side. About 150 employees, almost all of them young women, perished when the fire swept through the upper floors of the loft building in which they worked. Many burned to death; others jumped and died. Why so large a casualty list? The safety exits on the burning floors had been securely locked, allegedly to prevent "loss of goods." New York and the country were aroused by the tragedy. A state factory investigation committee headed by Frances Perkins (she was to become Franklin Roosevelt's secretary of labor in 1933, the first woman cabinet member in history) paved the way for many long needed reforms in industrial safety and fire prevention measures.

In November 1935, John L. Lewis announced the creation of the CIO, the Committee for Industrial Organization, composed of about a dozen leaders of AFL unions to carry on the effort for industrial unionism. Industrial Unions are unions that organize an entire industry regardless of skill. In short, they were unions of unskilled workers. In 1938, the CIO held its first constitutional convention and became the Congress of Industrial Organizations. The CIO began a remarkably successful series of organizing campaigns, and over the next few years, brought industrial unionism to large sectors of basic American industry. At the same time, the unions remaining in the AFL registered even more substantial gains in membership. During World War II, the AFL and CIO, while preserving areas of disagreement, began to find more substantial bases for working together on problems affecting all workers. The stage was set for merger of the two labor groups. They united into the AFL-CIO at a convention in New York that opened on December 5, 1955.

The AFL-CIO merger and its accompanying agreements brought about the virtual elimination of jurisdictional disputes between unions that had plagued the labor movement and alienated public sympathy in earlier years. The unions placed a new priority on organizing workers in areas, industries, and plants where no effective system of labor representation yet existed. In many cases, it meant crossing the barriers of old thinking and tired methods to reach the employees of companies that, for years, had resisted unions.

Thursday July 28, 2011

I'm in Kansas City. Another good day in class - I learned there is so much I do not know technically. It is just very complex equipment. The reassuring thing is that I am not alone. Talking to the other techs from all over the country, I found out they go through the same bullshit that I have been writing about. Our instructor drove us through the old

TRACK World headquarters campus. It was like a college campus, parking decks, beautiful all brick buildings, and a huge clock tower; really a striking place and it's all empty. The amount of money spent had to be staggering. In twenty years, it came and went. All gone; as a result of the long term visionaries and well educated management. I think it's sad.

Besides protecting workers, unions keep the corporate world accountable and I can't think of a better example than the Airlines pilot union and the players union in professional Football Basketball and Baseball. However corporate accountability to us commoners is becoming a thing of the past. As a customer and an employee now it seems that performance based compensation are the only source of accountability for executives and that strictly means that they continue to receive their dividends on a regular and increasing basis.

For the past forty years, there has been a steady decline in both union membership and influence across the country. There are several reasons for such a decline, the first having to do with employers keeping their businesses union-free. Some were active in their opposition and even hired consultants to devise legal strategies to combat unions. Other employers put workers on the management team by appointing them to the board of directors or establishing profit-sharing plans to reward employees. The second reason for union decline is that new additions to the labor force have traditionally had little loyalty to organized labor. Because more and more women and twenty something's are working and their incomes tend to be a family's second income or a starting salary they have a proclivity towards accepting lower wages, thus defeating the purpose of organized labor.

The third and possibly the most important reason for the decline in unions is that they are victims of their own success. Unions raised their wages substantially above the wages paid to nonunion workers. Therefore, many union-made products have become so expensive that sales were lost to less expensive foreign competitors and nonunion producers. This resulted in companies having to cut back on production, which caused some workers to lose their jobs, and hence, unions some of their members.

Monday (Labor Day) September 5, 1999

4:00AM - It's just cool working on this equipment. Standing next to these towers, I can't believe I am doing this. For years, I have looked at these towers and said, "Man, how cool would it be to work on that stuff?"

10:40AM I dosed off briefly but I am so spun up I cannot get to sleep. I can't get work out of my head. That is what sucks with this "on call." In my mind, it's like when I was a duty NCO in the Marines. I do not sleep soundly because subconsciously "I am on duty", or in this case, listening for my PDA to go off. This is brutal. I took a Xanax. I pray nothing happens today. I still have a boatload of shit to do in the office. I have to figure my hours for last week. I bet it is over 80. Hell yesterday was sixteen.

*7:40PM - Some of the techs I work with turn their phones off and I am starting to understand why. If you don't, you get harassed. What hurts is that I cannot call them for assistance. I was sifting through two months of emails in my inbox and I found the Workload Optimization Initiative document. The title alone is a euphemism. Line 1 says **"adherence"** and the fifth line item openly states **"enforcement."** This screams for union. Take a look:*

Agreed on commitments:

1. Starting the 13thof June 1492, all FSO L10s, Field Techs and dispatchers will "adhere" to the attached ways of working.

2. The L15 Access team members "will deliver ways of working" within their respective areas to all L5s and will ensure all Field techs receive communication regarding their new responsibilities.

3. The L15 Access team members will also act as POCs for their respective teams.

4. Software workload optimization deployment team will meet weekly Friday's at 09:00PDT.

*5. Dispatch management team will "**enforce**" the new ways of working nationally.*

6. All L15s can leverage L10 Core team members to address issues / concerns around the new ways of working and discuss with Dispatch management.

The last time someone told me "I will" do something was when I was in the Marines. And I'm not fond of the term "leverage" either as it is synonymous with "extort." Line 2 speaks of "new responsibilities." I'm still fixing cellular equipment, right? As I stated in my forward other then armed rebellion I believe unions are the only protection against this type of tyranny.

Our Trouble tickets are assigned priorities 1-5 which equates to repair time: A Priority 1 the highest with a one hour turnaround and priority 3 with eight hours. The problem is all the parties referenced in the above document have no technical skills when it comes to cellular networks and are in incapable of competent assessments. The reality is "priorities" and other variables are only assigned with the sole purpose to manipulate the SLA's. The subsequent data is really of null value because it's all manufactured and skewed; it's not real. I call it the "strip club correlation." Executives' come to a meeting and one party pretends the data is "valid" and the other party pretends to believe it. It is like a stripper: "she pretends to like you, and you pretend to believe her."

To me this Optimizing the Workforce entry is a real insight and demonstrates how upper level executives and leaders absolve themselves from accountability and reality. They are manipulating contrived statistics for a desired and predetermined out come. What happens to me or you is irrelevant. It is exactly why health Ins executives can take all the money while the doctors and nurses saving lives don't get shit or…how you invade a country for WMD's that don't exist? They're in a virtual world; it's not real…like a strip club! If you really examine what's happening with the "workforce optimization" I'm in the tangible fixing and or trouble shooting cellular networks and management is in the abstract manipulating bogus numbers. We are world's apart, heck I might as well be on Mars…which would be fine if I am with the Local Martian Telecomm 81.

The relationship between corporate management and unions has been a pendulum. At the turn of the 20th century, it swung in favor of business. After World War II and into the 80's, it was the unions' turn to be top dog. Now, it has greatly turned in favor of business. Again, I say that all you have to do is look at where our country is right now, and decide if this has been a good thing. If you are in the top 10% of earners in the United States, you are probably on the "Unions Are Evil" bandwagon. If you make up the rest of us working stiffs, you wonder when relief will come.

I believe we are so divided as a nation we are all ready in a cold civil war. Personally I think it is just a matter of time before we take up arms and history repeats itself. However, given our current state of segregation one would think the idea of union in any form would be welcomed. In fact, I believe the very act of opposition gives credence to the union movement because it recognizes their power and exposes the opposition for being oligarchs. Let me end with a passage from Hamilton Nolan, American writer:

"If workers cannot turn to the government to protect them from the unrestrained predations of corporate capitalism, then workers must find a way to protect themselves. Unless they plan to plunder the places they work for guns and start the revolution, then their best tool is a union. A strong union of workers, standing together, is in a position to bargain with a company, because a company needs employees in order to make money. Employees, alone, are in no position to bargain with a company, because employees need to eat."

Addendum: October 17, 2014

I watch Fox news and I just saw a piece with Eric Bolling about Wal-Mart employees protesting for $15.00 hour pay being backed by unions. To me he came across as rather pompous subtlety demeaning them as unskilled and clearly taking the anti-union stand. I am not trying to argue they are entitled to a life of privilege but everyone can't be an over achiever. Personally I believe everyone should be paid enough to cover all the insurances the "law" says I have to have. If we have to lower the maximum wage, so be it! However what set me off was his comparison to the Military and being shot at. I found myself yelling at the TV "Exactly! Enlisting in the military and being shot at is a better career option than working for Wal-Mart"

OP-ED I wrote about Unionizing Fast food workers. I emailed it out to papers all over the country. I have no idea if it was ever published. Here is a golden opportunity for corporate to participate in trickledown economics, stimulate the economy and help save middle-class America, but NOO! We have bunch of fat gluttonous executives lying around oozing cholesterol like Jabba the Hutt moaning *"more, I need more!"*

We can't unionize fast food, because Mr. Biggles is a Share Holder!

Fast-food workers are on strike and trying to unionize. Good for them! To me this coincides with the shrinking middle class which is because trickledown economics is a myth. Add to this a nation so segregated with greed we have blamed American Airlines for taking part in 9-11. And all economic statistics prove is that "data" is bull manure.

I believe trickledown economics is a myth. It may have had some credence in the 80's with Reagan, but not anymore. The theory is there are "ethics" in fiscal policy that in turn allows wealth to flow through the economy. Today there are no moral principles when it comes to finances as they can't be quantified.

Today we are far too polluted with greed and the arrogance of everybody else wants to live "my dream." There was a time when fast food work was really a starter job, a stepping stone. That went along with the promise of a future. There is no hope anymore and the reality is its becoming a career. The corporate officers of these fast food empires as well as in other sectors know it. They justify their actions by blaming the ambiguous entity called the "share holders." It reminds me of my 4 year old nephew when asked "how did this happen?" and would reply "it was Mr. Biggles"

The other argument we here from corporate is "We have a fiduciary agreement." Exactly! It's an agreement...not a law. But I'll even give them that one. Looking at the share holder argument again the stock market as we all know can be summed up in two words, "long term." So to say "I have to make the most amount of money right this minute" is not applicable: and as an afterthought where was all this concern for the shareholder in 2008? Their opposition to livable wages or to unions is just more evidence of capitalism consuming itself with "corporate" gluttony and all the more reason to unionize. If the business *"leaders"* were really *"leading"* as I'm sure they all have *"LEADERSHIP"* accolades plastered all over their office walls... then we wouldn't be having this argument now would we?

And to hear "my data says the glass is half full" and then to hear "my data says the glass is half empty." Pretty much speaks for itself. To make the argument that unions and wage increases are not beneficial because my statistics or data say's so...are well you know what I think? Personally I think unions are the only weapon for what's left of the middle class.

And let me add one last thing; who! Passes laws, talking to you! Elected officials, that states I will have to pay for all these insurances, meaning automobile and now health and doesn't pass a law saying I will paid enough to cover it? Seriously! WTF... how do you make that argument?

Chapter 10

Metrics...because that's all that matters

Thursday, May 26, 2011

Oh, but today it gets better. We have our weekly meeting and one of the issues discussed is how whoever is on call will create bogus tickets to cover time if they have not been called out. They do this in fear of not looking busy. Then when a real ticket or network issues arises, they have to address the bogus tickets. This causes them to work late and bill OT. I got into an angry debate with a co-worker. I said, "I am not creating bogus tickets because that's not in my realm of thinking." My co-worker said, "It's all about metrics. If you have time not accounted for, then you'll be gone." I said, "Fine! Send me to a market where the work is!" This kind of shit just infuriates me. Apparently being on call is not good enough. Management has to get even more metrics out of you. All these SLA's (Service Level Agreements) it is all so counterproductive.

I have heard missing an SLA is a huge deal and they end up with very heated meetings in upper management. I wonder if the real pressure about SLA's is not missing them, but rather, not being creative enough to come up with bullshit to circumvent and fudge the metrics so you don't miss the SLA in the first place because that's what really happens when it comes to SLA's.

The way I see it, we are being paid for our certifications, experience, market knowledge, education, military service, pride, loyalty! All the "intangibles" we bring to the table.

Things that can't be quantified and "metrasized" (I just made that word up) and don't generate "revenue." FUCKING deal with it! If you really think about it, you do not want me working because if I am working that means your network is fucked up. Other then scheduled maintenance we should be like the Maytag repairman: remember him? He was always bored because nothing ever broke, he sat on his ass! Management with all their education and superior intellect...just cannot seem to grasp this simple concept? It's astounding...

Nothing brought my morale down to a level lower then whale shit more than the constant garbage that went on with maintaining our level of working on ticket SLA's (Service Level Agreements). When I was in the service, there were some screwy things I put up with in terms of procedures and making sure everything was in its place, but the Marines paled in comparison to the telecom industry. As you can tell by this entry, the emphasis was to fudge metrics with bogus tickets while being "on-call" because that has become more important than actually keeping the network up and running.

I do not know all of the pressures put on my managers from their managers, but my company seemed to illustrate the point that all they want is metrics. I think we were a case study when all of the decisions made from above are centered on that one criterion with no real input from the men and women down below, then the ensuing results are less than optimal.

I believe most of my fellow technicians approached the job with the same mindset I had. Get to the problem at hand and fix or solve it. When you have good workers doing this, do you really want to make them cheat the repair process because of some artificial scoring system you set up to bullshit your customers? Instead of establishing procedures that would strengthen the company, management put

111

emphasis on numbers that force the work to be done in an unrealistic amount of time. When speed is the important driver, more problems occur. Do you remember that saying: If I spent more time doing things correctly the first time, I would not have to do them again the second time. Or even better "measure twice, cut once."

I understand how in business, things need to be quantified; numbers do tell a story, I get it but now its "database administrators and developers gone wild!" If management thinks they tell the entire story, then they have a screw loose. When I tackle a job management has no business telling me it should take X amount of time. The place may have been difficult to find, there may be more problems I found upon arrival, or I may have had to clear snakes or yellow jackets just to get near the equipment (all have happened). Hell I have been dispatched to sites that no longer exist! The point is there are many variables for each job that no one can predict which is what I enjoy about the work. When you become a slave to the numbers you are just that! You are disconnected to the true nature of the work.

Tuesday June 14, 2011

I resolved a ticket and I received another about an hour away. I do not know how to check IDEN (the push to talk) sites remotely so I had to drive to it. On arrival, I looked at the site log and a tech from a closer market (Charlotte) had been there and noted the error. He did not replace the bad part because he did not have one. I checked my truck and I did not have the required module either, so it was a wasted trip. I resolved my ticket "incomplete" and was going to contact dispatch via IM to make sure no other tickets were available before I drove the hour back to my market. Of course, I received the Blue Screen of Death on my computer. I "rolled the dice" anyway and took off towards home. I was half way back when I received another ticket and it was for the market which I had just left. As they say in Vegas "crap dice!" so I had to turn a around.

I received some interesting feedback from being on call last week. It was about all the hours I had documented. Apparently, we want to "not" dispatch as much as possible. I get it: don't roll out to a site if you don't have to. The dispatches I went on were for outages and I could not verify them remotely because they won't give me access to the software so I had to go. I cannot just blow things off. Otherwise I'm getting chewed out for a site being down and missing a SLA. Is this the most dysfunctional operation you have ever seen? It screams for union.

Ironic – I go out on service calls and they are happier if I do not go out and make service calls. I still have trouble wrapping my head around that one. Again, it all comes down to metrics and how they track and rate our performance. It is all about the quantity of "metrics" and little to do with actual quality. There were way too many times that I was urged to "park" a ticket so it would get off the board for the day. It did not matter if it was reopened tomorrow and I or some other grunt schmuck had to deal with it later with less time. All that mattered is that it was dealt with and management had more to manipulate. Is this any way to run a multi-billion dollar company?

Let me tell you a story. After World War II, Japanese industry was devastated. America, being the good sports that we are, invited their manufacturing leaders over to watch how we did things in some of our manufacturing arenas, especially in the auto industry. At that time, in the late 1940's and 50's, manufacturing plants in the USA took great pains monitoring quality control in just about everything made. The Japanese have always been a great people for paying attention to things that worked well, and to emulate them in their country. Their manufacturing people took their American lessons to heart and implemented many of our manufacturing practices in their country.

Fast-forward to the 1980's. Japanese car manufacturers are kicking our ass. Their cars are built better, more are sold, and Detroit is in a panic. Why? Because the Japanese took our quality control lessons as gospel while the American auto manufacturers got fat and happy. At the direction of management it was more important to pump out as many makes and models as possible. Auto executives figured they pretty much had the market in our country cornered, and it was not necessary to worry about things like how well the cars were built. It was a real management strategy and they called it "planned obsolescence." This all happened because carmakers were more worried about how many cars were sold; not necessarily how well they were made.

Thursday June 23, 2011 8:00AM

Last night started out with the usual chaos and confusion. First ticket I received was at 6:30PM which I have to accept and my shift starts at 9:00PM? It was for a site in another state. You can reject the ticket but they have a policy "we don't reject tickets". If you do dispatch immediately calls your manager and then he calls you. I had to call in to dispatch and inform them. Then I received two more tickets both of which were a two-hour trip in opposite directions. I think one came back a hundred and fifty miles away. I called dispatch and got into a heated discussion. He said to just park them and it took a minute to sink in. He was trying to get me to accept it by saying, "just park it." Problem is that now I am ultimately responsible for that ticket. So, we're making up bullshit terms like "park." If I did not "park" the ticket, he would call my manager and I would be harassed and bullied. Therefore, I accepted the tickets hoping I would not get thrown under the bus later.

My PDA or ticketing app was malfunctioning again. I finally had dispatch create me a ticket for going back to the site I was on the other night. I punched the circuit down and reconnected the router on our side so when the LEC (Local Exchange Carrier) makes the repairs on their part of the circuit, we "SHOULD?" be able to turn it up remotely without someone having to go back. That is the thought anyway? Some forward thinking that will be punished.

The other ticket was to verify copper theft. It is a big problem. The copper grounding bars are worth a couple hundred dollars and are always being stolen. Other than a security guard, I don't know what they can do to stop it.

Saturday August 6, 2011,

I just saw in the news a Boeing CH-47 Chinook military helicopter was shot down transporting a quick reaction force attempting to reinforce an engaged unit of Army Rangers in Afghanistan. The resulting crash killed all 38 people on board—

I just hope all these men were not put on one helicopter because of fuel "metrics?"

Addendum: Metrics the Curse on the middle class

Metrics are not a problem in and of its self. The difficulty happens when it becomes the final determination of anything and everything. Numbers can be easily manipulated. "Your metrics say the glass is half full, and my metrics say the glass is half empty." In almost any example, your expert can take numbers and makes them illustrate your point. Then I can get my expert to take those same numbers and show something the complete opposite.

While corporations are very good at manipulating their numbers for their advantage, Washington DC has raised this to an art form. Our government leaders can use numbers to prove their point – no matter how much they need to manipulate or highlight them. Let's take a minute and look at what they do with unemployment numbers. The folks in Washington cheer because, according to their numbers, the percentage of people now unemployed is near what it was before the economy went to hell in 2008. The problem is, their conversation stops there. They do not want to acknowledge all the numbers. After all, unemployment has been a huge problem that has fractured the foundation of our country. However, the "truth" is that the downturn that began 6½ years ago, accelerated wrenching changes that have left many Americans feeling worse off than they did the last time the economy had roughly the same number of jobs as it does now.

There are still millions of construction jobs missing. Factories have fewer workers. Many of these jobs have been permanently replaced by new technologies: robots, software and advanced equipment that speeds productivity and require less manpower. Government payrolls have shrunk, taking middle class pay with them. Active duty military are now being handed pink slips on the battle field or being encouraged to leave with buy outs. Local school districts have fewer employees. The U.S. Postal Service has shed 194,700 employees. And during the economic recovery, more people have left the job market than entered it. A lot of people have given up: and I wonder? Do they have a metric for suicides?

For an economy that too often seems to use the surging stock market as a barometer, the bottom 30 percent of workers earn wages, that when adjusted for inflation, have fallen over the past 14 years. Three generally low-paying industries account for more than one-third of the job gains in the recovery: restaurants and bars, temporary staffing, and retail according to research by the National Employment Law Project. Pay in these sectors averages under $13.34 an hour.

Another reality of today is that more than 27.2 million Americans now work part-time, about 2.5 million more than before the recession. Roughly, a quarter of those workers would prefer to be full time according to surveys. And while the number of full-time workers has risen during the 5-year-old recovery, the economy still has 2.9 million fewer of them.

As you can see, there are things to be gathered looking at the metrics of a situation, and then there is truth. Corporate America, like the American government, will go out of its way to avoid the truth. The problem is that truth does not just go away. We are in a parallel situation in America between business and government. They can either look at all the numbers or figure out a way to make things better for everyone, or they can continue burying their head in the sand and wait for Armageddon.

Calibrations, I really enjoyed these, I got to work at night by myself, and it involved everything from a power drill to my laptop. That is a test set bottom right used to calibrate the RF frequencies with a Vendor application connected to my laptop. The test set was old and way overdue on its calibration date but management did not want to pay to have calibrated. Often I would have to reboot it several times as it would crash.

"You can ignore reality, you just can't ignore the consequences of ignoring reality." ~ Ayn Rand

Chapter 11

Communication from a communication company, who knew?

12:15AM Thursday June 9, 2011

Holy shit! It has been an eighteen-hour shift. I could keep working if I wanted to. So many processes, so many different types of equipment, tools, applications and support numbers, it is daunting. When I call for support and ask questions everyone seems so uncertain. There is never a definitive answer. This industry is just wrought with ambiguity. You can look right at "GREEN" LED's on an I/O card that supposed to tell you it's good but if you replace it the errors coming from the site and causing alarms go away, so it was really a bad card AHHH! On the other hand, you may not catch errors because your test equipment is not calibrated. You think everything is fine. You sign off on a ticket and then an hour later you get a phone call and a manager from somewhere says, "Hey! Half the state is down and you were the last one on site."...It really happens.

Picture yourself attending your first Indy car race. As you go through the gates, the attendant scans your ticket and tells you, "You are the grand prize winner today! You get to drive one of the cars in today's race." Before you know what is happening, two guys grab you by the arms and take you down to the track. You do not even get a chance to look around and before you know it, you are zipped into racing coveralls, a helmet is shoved onto your head, and you are wedged into the cockpit of a highly sophisticated Indy-style racing machine. The flag drops, and you are zipping away in the middle of a race at 200 mph with a death grip on the steering wheel. No preparation and no training, just go. Hell, nobody even asked you if you had a driver's license!

That is a little bit of what it was like to start working with my company. I often felt like I was on a Marine training exercise where they give you a knife, drop you off in the middle of nowhere, and tell you, "See you back at the base." In fairness to the Marines, though, they do not do that until you have some training under your belt.

On the other hand, I work for a multi-billion dollar telecom company that sees nothing wrong with extensive on-the-job training...by yourself. I will be the first to say that when it comes to technology, the best way to learn is "hands on." Most companies or organizations want you to do well and will give you the guidance in the form of an apprenticeship to help make sure that comes to fruition. I never felt like I worked for one of the "most" companies! Case in point, when I was sent into a declared disaster to set up a generator...area by myself.

I have talked a little before about our managers and the lack there of. There were exceptions of course, but it seemed like the number one rule of management in my company was CYA – Cover Your Ass and "we are not going to pay for anything." That kind of approach gives your workforce less than a warm, fuzzy feeling. It is my theory that most workers are like me: they do not need or want to be micromanaged. We have been screened via the hiring process and we are professionals. A good manager with personal experiences in the trade will be behind the scenes almost covertly helping them to perform their jobs by providing and anticipating anything and everything. After all, if a manager is judged on the work I do, shouldn't he or she make sure I am equipped and knowledgeable for my job? The time to find out that I am not trained or I am not equipped with the proper tools is not when half the state has lost network access and dispatch is calling with a "director escalation"?

That is what I meant in my entry above when I said, "This industry is just wrought with ambiguity." The technology alone to make a cellular network process your calls is mind numbingly complex. When the people who are supposed to manage it and make the advisory decisions seem more than a little vague in knowing what is going on it just makes a all ready complicated condition worse.

I think many times bosses and managers get to their positions for the wrong reasons; in fact I know it! "We rise to our level of incompetence" ~ The Peter Principle. For instance, Lisa may have a Bachelor in Business Admin and a wiz at "metrics" with numbers or be certified in "Project Management". But if she has never worked in the cellular industry or utilized the tools...she has no clue how to lead or communicate within the trade. How do you "manage" something you know nothing about? You don't, why... because, "reality trumps positive thinking" and all the education and certifications will never change that.

Thursday August 4 2001 1:20PM

I just woke up, so I decided to write while I wait for a Lorazepam to kick in so I can go back to sleep. I received a call from my manager this morning about a ticket I closed the other night as NTF (no trouble found). I remember it because there was no information in the ticket. It just said, "sweep the antenna lines." I told him "all it said was sweep lines." That would require taking the entire site down and it will take far more time than is allotted in the ticket duration to set up all the test equipment. Was it for voice, data, a sector...dropped calls well that's a given! What was the problem? Why am I sweeping the lines? I am looking for basic information in the ticket, something to give me a direction to start trouble shooting. Furthermore, my suspicion is this came from the RF guys as a retaliation for getting buried in work due to the fact that the new guy (aka yours truly) is performing calibrations at night which quadruples their work load in the day. But I could never say that…Stay tuned.

During our conversation, my manager stated like it was the accomplishment of a life time, "Well, I am on the committee for investigating tickets that are closed with "no trouble found" when apparently there is a problem and this is in my market." I immediately thought to myself, "So now management is ganging up on us!" I really felt that way and as I contemplated some more I thought…"So the automated ticketing and work force software now needs an entire committee to intervene in the automation?" yet there are only two field techs supporting half the state?

I really wanted to say "why don't pull your head out of your committee and come help us in the field. You know we are under manned" That's the fundamental problem here. How do you NOT know that? You're trying to support 26,000 cell sites 24/7 with 1400 field techs; do the math! Oh wait…they did! And now these dumb fucks form a committee?

What a good manager should have done in this case was not read me the riot act. He could see all the meta data in the ticket including who or how it originated. He should have investigated up the line to determine why so little information was in the ticket. He could even raise the bar and score brownie points examining what is going on within the entire company that warrants the need for a committee? Obviously something is happening to suddenly make so many field techs close tickets NTF? I guess that meant he would have had to think things through and take the initiative

122

to actually solve a problem aka "communicate" but NOO! It was more important for him to be on a "committee."

Thursday September 1, 2011 4:30PM

I was woken up from a sound sleep by a phone call from a CM Customer Management Rep. He was apologetic, but I told him it is fine since I am on-call. He told me that a customer has been having roaming problems. I knew about this because I had been assigned this ticket this morning and was aware but I have been working for 20 hours straight and I told dispatch that I needed to get some sleep before taking it on. If he is calling, then it is a big deal in fact he said it had been escalated to director level. (I hate that fucking word "escalation"...if they had enough people staffed in the first place you wouldn't have to "escalate!") All I am interested in is the technical aspects. He started to try to explain things I cut him off and said "What are the POC (Point of Contact) numbers?" as they can really tell you what's going on...or not. He said I have two numbers and two names: Joe and Frank. I said, "That's fine. I will get right on it."

As soon as we hung up, I called the POC. I said, "I have been told you are having trouble. Can you give me some information as to what the specific problem is?" The first gentleman I spoke with was very vague. He was stuttering a bit and when I started pressing him technically he said, "I will let you talk to my network guy." I'm thinking great! Now I have to talk to some techno geek who jerks off while he writes code, and probably knows a lot more than I do, but I have to do my job. Regardless, I do want to help the customer. As we start talking, he mentions things like "all over" and "everywhere I go." I politely ask him, "Is this at your present office location, correct?" Then he starts to open up. "We have calls dropping everywhere we travel. I have had this discussion with our account rep." I had to do everything in my power not to say, "Are you nuts! You listened to an account rep?"

Instead, I said, "Your current location is working, correct?" He said, "Yes." I said, "OK, so you are having problems with your service everywhere. I am sorry to hear that. I am a technical person they notified. If you thought it would do any good I would be more than willing to come out there." He said, "You can if you like to perform your due diligence, but everything is fine here in our building." I tried to smooth the situation and think I said something like, "Well you know us worker bees. We're just down here in the trenches." something to let him know I could empathize. Again I felt like screaming, "I AGGRE! And I know why exactly why your service really sucks! It's because management thinks they can support the whole state with two field techs...and I am keeping a journal to write a book about it and this is gonna be in it!"... I did not of course.

I called the CM back and told him about our discussion. His first comment to me was, "Gee, I am glad you called them." I wanted to say, "Yeah, what a concept communication from a communication company?" I did say, "I think they just want out of their contact. They are dissatisfied with their service, that's what they are after." I resolved the ticket with no site visit required.

Sometimes I marvel how the United States is the most successful capitalistic country on earth. Yet we have so many people in charge of businesses and organizations who could not run a lemonade stand. Whether someone is the top dog or part of an executive leadership team or a low level manager aka "boss" having a position of authority does not automatically endow a person with wisdom: another argument for the unions as they tend to manage themselves.

The current economic state validates this statement. Psychologist and workplace intervention expert, Michelle McQuaid, conducted a study of one-thousand people. The study showed bad bosses can cost the economy $360 billion annually in lost productivity. McQuaid says three out of every four people report the most stressful part of their day is dealing with their boss. I have to say Ms. McQuaid is correct and she never even interviewed me!

```
* 9/25/2012 2:35 PM, RA03XC032, Waiting Internal, [-1]
* 9/26/2012 8:14 PM, RA03XC123, Waiting Internal, [-1]
* 7:25 PM, RA33XC268, Accepted, [-1]
* 7:33 PM, RA03XC042, Dispatched, Jeopardy - Not Accepted
* 9/28/2012 2:45 PM, RA03XC040, Waiting Internal, [-1]
* 9/28/2012 5:38 PM, RA33XC252, Dispatched, Jeopardy - Not Accepted
* 10/1/2012 9:30 AM, RA21XC310, Waiting Internal, [-1]
```

My Work Force Software interface and my tickets in queue, notice ticket at 7:25PM Accepted, 7:33PM Dispatched, and in Jeopardy, it's from a game show host? We were not allowed to reject tickets even though it was a option in the software.

There are many factors that contribute to a bad boss. We'll focus on two– the first of which is when an individual is promoted to a leadership position for the first time. What often happens in a company is that somebody does great in their job whether it is in corporate sales, doing marketing, conducting research, selling on the department store floor, etc. That person is then thrust into the position of supervising others usually the same people they used to work alongside. This can cause problems in of itself because it tends to create animosity. The military deals with this by transferring people however this is usually not an option in the civilian world. If a person has never had any leadership opportunities in any capacity, they are going to flounder. What ends up happening is that they are going to try to be a boss like one of their supervisors…who may be equally inept at the job because they also did not have a clue about what they were doing. It is like someone who becomes a parent for the first time and repeats all of the mistakes that his or her parents did. It is the only example they have ever had.

Another problem occurs when a person believes that since he is the boss or manager, he can do no wrong. This type of person feels that they have the perfect right to be king and do whatever they want. This arrogance can lead to disaster and can cost a company a great deal in money and time buy creating disgruntled workers and a high turnover or even worse violence in the work place. What is that saying, "Pride goeth before the fall"?

There is a huge difference between being a leader and a boss. This is the distinction that people have to recognize and then make an effort at learning. Being in charge means possessing a combination of skills in organization, communication, psychology, goal orientation, and a particular knowledge of whatever the business is and what the workers do. Not just being "educated" with the ability to extrapolate data and read spread sheets. Leaders observe and motivate by being hands on with the ability and desire to empathize and thus communicate effectively with anyone including having the balls to say "NO we're not gonna do that and here is why."

To me very few people have an innate talent and ability for leadership. The good news is that everyone can learn the necessary skills but this only comes from a long term application or in corporate vernacular a "low turnover." Of course, training only works if a person approaches it with an open mind and attitude. And this usually comes from knowing one is likely to have their job for a while; also known as…all together now "LOW TURNOVER!"

Chapter 12

Reality Is Counter-Productive to Virtual Reality

Wednesday August 3, 2011 7:35PM

Interesting meeting this morning with our director this morning. It was follow up to a mandatory all-hands call in I had to attend or sit in a conference room staring at a speaker phone. The VP spoke about a manager and what's going on with being sold to SWEDEN. Prior to my arrival some disgruntled tech had recently carpet bombed the entire company with an email slamming his manager while expressing all his thoughts and opinions about management. Normally IT departments have their email servers configured specifically so that cannot be done; But apparently not here? I think it is funny.

The director openly mocked the automated ticketing system. He said it was designed for use in Europe where they may have 300-400 cell sites and I believe he said we are trying to use it on 26,000 sites throughout the United States. He boasted of how he was one of sixty directors that kept his job and then joked how every time telecomm companies merge, they cut jobs. I envy him. How he can be so cavalier about almost losing his job or seeing your co-workers dismissed and their lives turned upside down?

On the surface, he seemed personable but doesn't everyone? I'll bet my left nut he was all doped up on some kind of meds, hell EVERYBODY IS! I am sure he has a family to support and enjoys life like the rest of us. That being said, does he take that into consideration when he looked right at us and addressed us as "resources" There was that word again! The amateur psychologist in me would love to know what goes through his mind to think that's acceptable. The arrogance and lack of humility in management just blows my mind. I have felt more respected when I was guest at the 81's club house.

Maybe I'll start a Union and our motto will be "You're not a resource, you're a person" Every now and then in my travels through the corporate world I would write that on a white board if I was in a conference room and no one was around.

My long-term goal is shifting from becoming a good tech and helping the customer to "how can I just get the fuck out of this insanity" I am falling back into just surviving the week and self medicating through the weekends. When I was hired I really, really looked at this job almost as gift; a genuine opportunity to embrace the future and put the past behind me. It's sad.

Thoughts: It often struck me in my time with SWEDEN, how many dumb things came out of the mouths of some of my supervisors. They probably did not think before putting their mouth in gear but they didn't have to. They got paid to lie and nowhere is it more rewarded than in the corporate culture. They bury reality with euphemisms and legal departments that blur lines while executives perfect the art of skewing metrics while pretending it's valid. Of course everyone is in therapy and on anti- depressant. It all becomes "Virtual" which by definition is "not real." Growing up in Jersey I learned to read between the lines and call someone out. Let's look at the above entry a little more in depth.

The obvious highlight of the conversation with my director is how we were using a ticketing system that was designed for about 12% of the size of our company's market. The other thing is we only have about 1400 techs. So you have 1400 people trying to support 26000 sites. You do not have to be an engineer or a bright person to know that this is just asking for problems. You have probably gathered from my journal entries that this is exactly what happened. When upper management knows it is a problem and, is openly mocking it, why don't you fix it or stop using it? Is it because that it will cut into the quarterly earnings of the stockholders and that is the holy grail of a corporation these days? It is just amazing how little time seems to be devoted to the long-term success of a company. I guess it's all part of our instant, quantified, Giga Bit, selfie, economy. Problem is what's the alternative if there is no more long term; short term and just keep getting shorter? My British friend from college, really bright guy, says its capitalism consuming itself...and democracy with it?

A good friend of mine was an Advertising Executive at a local TV network; and may he rest in peace. He used to tell me how companies always bitched about paying for advertising and would say "we don't need it, it's not worth it" until they were filing for bankruptcy and going under. What's the first thing they would do! Call him and start buying up all of his ad time for the "Going out of business sale." So much for long term vision but aren't these supposed to be educated and smart people? I mean I'm sure my director attended the center for creative leadership and his boss sits on the committee for strategic marketing...initiatives?

The other thing you can pick up here is how happy our director is with keeping his job. I mean, he should be. But there is something called karma, or the nation's economy that has shown everyone that what goes around comes around. The recession of 2008, and for the last one or two decades before that, has shown us that there is no loyalty anywhere in the corporate culture; it doesn't fit in a business model. This director could be out on his ass quicker than greased lighting.

You also do not want to tell your troops their worth to the company can be measured in nanoseconds. What am I supposed to infer when I here *"telecomm companies merge, they cut jobs?"* I have worked my butt off for all of these long shifts and driving around like I'm in death race 2000 and they can still give me a pink slip anytime. I guess that's the key take away? Still it doesn't make sense when cellular networks and smart phones are proliferating like the Catholics.

It is dehumanizing to be called a "resource." The implication is I'm only here to be disposed of. Yet I am sure my director believes we are supposed to be optimistic about our future? Yes a future as a "resource" sounds promising? I guess that's his reality; and the power of anti depressants? Coal is a resource and come to think of it, maybe it is a good comparison. After all, coal is thrown into the fire, creates energy, burns up and then it's gone. Yup, sounds like my job description to the "T."

The last thing you probably learned from this is that I had to get hammered on weekends to keep my sanity. Not exactly the healthiest lifestyle but neither is being a resource. Hmm but maybe if I could look at it with a management perspective…yeah that's it, positive thinking! "It's better for me to abuse drugs and alcohol then let drugs and alcohol abuse me."

Wednesday February 4, 2012

Got an email today about "work place violence" and how it will not be tolerated.

REALLY! As opposed to "team we need to meet our work place violence allocation before end of fiscal year?"

What really upsets me is I read this to be an admission by management they have created a hostile work environment and they are blatantly aware and subsequently worried about it. Why else would anyone send out an email like this? I want to know where is all the concern for the physical duress inflicted on me when management denies me sleep or I am harassed and bullied into accepting more tickets after working 13 hours for 15 days straight and I'm exhausted. I wonder if I punched my manager if I could use this email in court as a "defense." "you see your honor I took this email to mean management wanted proof they had created a hostile work environment so I took the initiative...I mean John Wayne would have hit him."

Tuesday August 23 7:00PM

As you now know, I get automated tickets sent to me. I complete them as fast as I can because I try to be a good employee; it is my job, my work ethic, it's how I work. I don't really pay attention to durations they make no sense to me because every trouble call is unique that's what I like about this job. I was told by my lead tech, "Well, you shouldn't do that." He was telling me not to close tickets to early. For one he said you won't get credit for it and the other was it makes everyone else look bad. He didn't say it in a threatening manner. He was just making me aware. Wait for the prescribed duration and he was right. What happens is management will want to know why other techs aren't closing tickets sooner. It just reiterates how stupid the whole idea is of putting durations on tickets.

Earthquake today! Woke me right up I have never been in one. At first I thought it was the neighbors "doing it!" No lie, but the apartment was really shaking. I saw the walls sway in and out. That was wild! I wonder if I was on site working...is there an earthquake metric?

Earthquakes on the east coast are rare. This is the one that originated in Virginia and did damage to the Washington Monument. Of course, people in California just laughed at it. They said that what we had would not even wake them up. I told someone "yeah! My reality is unstable enough...like I really need the ground shaking beneath my feet?" "Just call the men in the white suits."

Mixed messages at my job, go figure? I think this short journal entry summed up all of my frustrations in a few sentences. Whether it was playing lacrosse or being in the Marines, I have grown up with a sense of teamwork as it is a "reality" in the world of sports. There is real truth in saying that, "The strength of the wolf is in the pack, and the strength of the pack is in the wolf." If a group, in this case a company, really wants both the individual and the corporation to reach its heights, everything and everyone has to work together. You can't have some people in "virtual reality" everyone has to be in touch with "reality reality."

Unfortunately, a lot of the impression us grassroots workers received is that it was every man (or woman) for themselves. In this case it's the old "it's us against them" axiom. Meaning "us" the field techs have to not close tickets early for "them" management. Is this my reality for the rest of my days? Why can't I just go fix something and when I m done I'll go fix something else? The sorry truth is that this "enforcement" from managers and supervisors begins to squeeze out my teamwork belief. I mean, you can only be told to "stay positive and keep flapping your arms, it's for the team" so long before you realize you are not going to get off the ground.

I am not just talking from my basic belief system here. A popular training exercise when you are promoting teamwork is to give everyone a sheet of paper explaining that you are shipwrecked on an island. You are given a list of maybe 15 items you have with you, and you have to number those items to show what you think is most important down to the least important. Then you get broken down into groups and the group has to then prioritize those same items. What happens 98% of the time is that the group does a better job at prioritizing correctly than does the individual.

It is easy to see that this basic concept holds true in the workplace. Somewhere along the way, though, priorities get really screwed up. The emphasis when you are on shift becomes more of meeting the demands of the software than it does in really fixing things the best way possible. Do you see anything wrong with that; something to think about when you're listening to digital recordings of how you are "valued"...as a customer?

Sunday September 4, 2011

A long entry but see if you can stay with it.

3:00PM No ticketing app all day, it is down! I have had to call dispatch for everything. One of them was for dropped calls and I test drove the site while talking to my college buddy. It never dropped. I can see where the call "hands off" transfers to another tower as I drive and it worked smoothly.

8:30 PM - I received a call from the GNOC along with a ticket, or I should say a voice message, saying I was getting a ticket because the ticketing app is still down. It is a Golden BTS and it is bouncing. That is a high priority site and the SLA is three hours to repair. I cannot get a break. Therefore, I don my superman costume and like an idiot, I tell dispatch "just put me in progress." Normally you do not put yourself "in progress" until you get on site: this is all done in the ticketing application. But dumb ass me is thinking TADA!! "It is a Golden BTS. I want them to know I am on it." So that fucked me out of an hour on the SLA I think? On arrival I have to go through three gates with combination locks, four counting the cabinet below the tower. When I finally get into the equipment I pull a circuit breaker. Sure enough, it goes down. I push the breaker back in and it comes up and I watch it. After five minutes, it greens up and stays green. I am like awesome! I am the man. Call the GNOC and they verify it is up. I will monitor it for about fifteen or twenty minutes and then close the ticket and save the day.

Naturally, I am not that lucky. Sure enough, I see it go red. But one thing I can try is to take the whole site down. This means powering down every piece of equipment and then bringing them all back up sequentially. That is what I did. It all came up for about fifteen minutes and then red! Shit! Now I have to go back to the shop and pray we have the part I think is bad. I look at my documentation to make sure I am getting the right component. From the outside, some of the parts look the same. They are the same chassis but inside some handle data and others just voice. According to my docs, this piece is a combination voice and data. I pack up and lock up and just as I start to drive away, a thought occurs to me. Despite what my documentation tells me, I should go back and verify I am getting the right component. If there is one thing I have learned in all my years, "the only thing that is certain is that nothing is certain."

No lie - I could not get back into the entry gate, I just locked it! I thought I was losing my mind or was I in the twilight zone! I tried WD-40 and I could see I only changed one number. I ended up using my bolt cutters and cut the lock off.

I get back to the cabinet and open it up. If you look very closely on the part number sticker in tiny print it says 1X-modem, which tells me it's a voice only component. My documentation was showing me data. Thank God, I went back to check. I would have ordered the wrong component.

As I am driving, I am thinking that technically this site is still providing data it's just the voice component that's broken so it is not really down and we may not be in violation of the SLA.

I install the new component, push the breaker, and wait. It is blinking red and then I am waiting some more. It goes green, but it is still blinking. I walk to back to the truck and smoke a cigarette and try to plan my next move if this does not fix it. I come back and its solid green. Yea! But will it stay solid green? ...Tada! it does!

Since cell phones are such a way of life, I think most people just take it for granted that they will work. This entry shows a little of the technology that goes on behind your phone. You can be driving in California speaking to someone driving in New York. The technology it takes to recreate your voice on the other side of the country while both parties are driving in opposite directions is very complex. It's just a fact of "reality" you need a skilled and knowledgeable workforce to maintain and support it; and enough of them! Sadly here is another area where we the technicians get taken advantage of because management only looks at us through software or their skewed "virtual reality" for the bottom line and not the reliability of a well maintained network.

I remember reading stories about the old Soviet Union. They always had a five-year plan for getting their economy going. One of the problems they had was the lack of initiative by their workers. For instance, if a farmer's tractor broke down, he was screwed. He had to wait until the designated tractor expert showed up to fix it. An American farmer, on the other hand, would play around with the engine until he got it started. He calls a mechanic only as a last resort and they may even work together on the repair. Our entire "industrial" history is based on people taking the initiative to get things going and "WORKING" to repair or improve them. It brought us the concept of having a "career" and a middle class. Now thanks to workforce software and managements insistence to quantify everything and everyone we have five people who only focus on ticket durations and one person left to perform the "real" work.

Tuesday September 20, 2011

1:40AM - I got into it with my manger again. I did not send the equipment in the inventory database to the right designation. He said, "I sent you an email and I told you." He was right but I can only take in so much information. I said, "You send fifteen emails a day marked urgent action Item or Required – Important. If I read all your emails I would never get out the door." But I backed off and said, "All right, I will handle it." He gave me the name of someone to call. I finally spoke to the woman who handles the database for our region. She said, "Oh, I recognize your name." I said, "Is that good or bad?" She said, "That's good. You email me and ask questions about the database, so I know you are using it." I told her "believe me I'm pretty tech savvy; I even built an Access database but I am afraid of this one, it befuddles me." She laughed. She was very helpful and said she will have to generate a report and see if she can do damage control. Whatever that means? She will get back to me in a few days. I can't wait?

I got sent to a site in another market and while I was there I ran into another tech. I told him where I was from and the very next topic was my manager and how he is known to be an asshole. He told me he gets maybe one email a day from his manager. I told him I must get twenty emails a day and I said I was looking forward to getting out of there.

Carriers adds went well. Doing the equipment installs has really paid off. I am getting to know all the equipment intimately because sometimes I crawl half way into the cabinets. It's like a game of twister to reach some of the parts; "twister" anyone remember that one?

Some people mistake activity for work. I think my manager firmly falls into this category. It seems to me that a good supervisor tries to alleviate roadblocks and extra work to streamline the efforts of those under him. Mine must have missed that memo. Of course, it was probably because he was too busy sending out so many of his own to "cover his ass" *Did you get the memo about the meeting? It was a meeting about the memos?*

It is rarely easy to do great in your job every day. With most work, including mine, there are so many variables that come into play. Faulty equipment, access issues, incorrect tools or receiving the wrong parts, or just bad timing. You know? When the "Murphy's" show up; unannounced! That's a reality we can all relate to at one time or another. The one thing that should not be a "constant" is where your own company "constantly" gets in the way of your success.

Chapter13

Is Management Clueless?

Monday July 25, 2011 9:16PM

I just got off from "on-call." Friday and Saturday were insane and I must have had a ticket every two hours. I was so busy and tired I did not have a chance to write. I was all over the place with outages and equipment failures. To top it off, I had to fly out Sunday morning to Kansas City and I am in the hotel as I write.

The course I am attending is a basic RF course. RF stands for Radio Frequency. I am pretty psyched because I have some experience and this is a nice break from work. I am in a classroom environment where I can ask questions and get instructions on the equipment I support. I am particularly weak on the electrical systems and the rectifiers that convert power from AC to DC. It is one of the pieces of equipment I am responsible for maintaining and trouble shooting. It should be a good course. When I got in last night, I was trying to complete my time. I know my manager always wants time done by Monday. Of course, I had to enter separate codes for traveling. I was delirious with exhaustion and needed some sleep. After about an hour of screwing with these stupid codes, I sent off the following message to my manager:

Bill, what codes do I use for travel in the time entry application, I assume the training code and travel. I saw this in an email: activity code 1120 and network code 91826733 when training and completing the courses on

line but this is course "in attendance" and I don't see that network code listed? I know if I don't get it right you will hit me up with a nasty gram so I am trying to get right. I have a suggestion. Why don't they just track every dollar by the serial number? That is about where we are at. I apologize, but as you can see, I get frustrated. I do not believe it should be this difficult every time I do something slightly different from the normal workweek. Anyway, please advise so I can submit my time. I am a little tired. They ran me ragged Friday and Saturday. I believe I had a ticket every two hours."

Was I being slightly sarcastic in my note? Definitely – but I wanted to get my point across. Is there a code for boarding the plane? How about a code for lunch, and a code for a Tuna Sandwich because that's what I had during the flight? It is absolutely insane. I should be able to enter 8 for eight, hours well in my case it's 15, for fifteen hours under "M" (Monday) and "T" for (Tuesday) and then rest of the week which goes W.T.F…Get it, WTF?

I know that documentation is the bane of almost every profession. Somewhere, there has to be a business definition for "intelligent administration." I guess that may be an oxymoron, but it is so desperately needed in industry today; especially for the guy doing the work. I am sure telecom is not the only business that makes life harder than it needs to be.

Here is what I think happens. Picture a long hallway with twenty offices. Each office has a certain responsibility for some operational component of the company. Shipping, HR, vendors, pay roll, operations, provisioning, IT, facilities, accounting, sales, test phones, security, legal, travel, etc. – you name it. One way or the other, the folks working the field (like yours truly) generate some activity that each of these offices have to keep track of. So they each create a database and subsequent code to track my functions. This system may work fine for each of them within their own little domain, but it makes my life a living hell. And I don't even want to get in to what happens when they start out sourcing? It becomes my other full time job performing data entry, review and correlation just so I can document my work to get paid. It actually is a real job and it is what's known as a "Systems Analyst"

Tuesday September 27, 2011 10:20AM

I have this fear their going to fire me because I lip off now and then. One time I got into it with my manager and he said "you're putting words into my mouth". I thought about it and my frustration lies in the fact that I have in way volunteered or put myself out here to work at night to do things that others do not want to do, as we used to say in the Corps that makes you the "tallest pole in the tent". There is no shame in that fact that I am new and learning. My manager knows I am new to all this. It's a difficult enough just supporting the RF equipment and the network I am all ready under tremendous stress so to continually pound on me about trivial issues knowing there are more important things to be addressed is amateur. But this is the guy who attends the University of Phoenix while we're surrounded by some of the best universities in the country and there is a "real" college every other mile all offering continuing education. How do these people get in management positions? Has anyone ever been denied admission to the University of Phoenix? How is one supposed to better themselves if there is no risk of failure? Anyways, I would think I would be provided more support as this should be a two man crew and it was at one time! I would think I would be provided more support. As I said this should be a two man job and it was at one time. One very experienced field tech and one newbie such as myself. It used to be that way. Continual rotation while teams work together. This is how you forge a team you cheap bastards not by putting motivational posters on the wall?

I can only say that last entry is some venting... I said in my forward I was frustrated and disappointed.

Sunday September 30, 2012

I received an email about an escalation from my manager. I found it strange because it was for scheduled maintenance. Escalations are normally for outages or something directly impacting a customer. It was for a T1 augmentation (a new installation) As soon as I saw the site ID, I knew right where it was - they call that market knowledge. I replied OTW! On my arrival, I opened the Telco box where the T1's are located and guess what? There was no circuit installed, nothing plain and simple. I took a picture and replied to my manager's email. All this shit over an empty box! I mean there was nothing in it. The LEC (local phone company) had not installed the circuit yet. I was escalated to an empty box. I was telling my mother and brother and they were laughing hysterically.

"ESCALATION." I HATE THAT FUCKING WORD. There was another time my manager called and told me, "You have a ticket that's about to be escalated. It's for running power." I said, "I have never run power. Oh wait a minute - I think I saw a video on how it is done. Guess I am now a licensed electrician?" Geez - you just let a tech go from our market I bet he could run power?

Come to think of it I don't think any of us were qualified on power. There was a time where you had electricians or techs really trained on power but of course they ran

141

them off. Besides electrocuting myself, I would probably shut down the power grid for the eastern seaboard! This was a typical form of harassment that we endured. We would be bullied into accepting a ticket or it would be "put on you" by a manager through the software. Heck, sometimes you would just login and see tickets with your name on it. I can tell you if you are at a site back in the woods by yourself; you could get killed if you did not know what you are doing. This is especially true if you were working with power. By the time they found you, you would be bird food. Hell, on second thought, they may never know you are gone because "missing tech" hadn't been written into the software yet.

When I read that last passage, it makes me wonder if I was being setup for failure or it was retaliation. I wouldn't put anything past my manager he was a complete dolt. If there is one thing I have seen throughout my entire professional career is the childish behavior of people in the work place; heck right on up to the president. Could you imagine if the intern stepped backwards; the leader of the free world would have been left standing there exposing himself? The antics of corporate executives who run around acting as if they are still in high school all while preaching standards of conduct and bestowing values is unreal? I cannot tell you how many times I would hear of some VP or director dumping his wife of twenty years for some young female admin or sales rep; thus giving her the option to quit the work force, not an option I have ever had but that's another story? In retrospect I think that's why I encountered resentment at work. I respect the institution of marriage enough to know it was not for me. I freely admitted to my immaturity, usually by talking about my weekend exploits about which I was usually asked about on Mondays by inquisitive co-workers, married of course, whom I'm sure used it against me if and when they could. I believe leadership and respect starts in the home. My parents loved, admired and respected each other; it was a team effort and how I was raised. I think it's a sad symptom of our fucked up priorities today but it seems children and marriage are looked at in typical corporate fashion; a short term quantified project with metrics and people you just outsource if you don't meet "projections?" To me if you can't manage your home then you can't manage me. I am sorry, as I have a lot of friends who are divorced but I believe it's about "being" married not "getting" married and a real "leader" will have the foresight to realize that and wait; I digress. Back to the "escalation" put on me by my manager. This was more like an "I have the mentality of a pre-pubescent school girl"...I don't like you, so I'm gonna retaliate any chance I can because "you put word's in my mouth?"

Friday March 9, 2012 1:20AM

More harassing E-mails from my manager about unfinished tickets and they just cut staff and let people go?

"Anger is merely depression with enthusiasm"...I just want to punch him!

Friday August 12,2011 9:00AM

I think my manager called me on purpose. "Heard you had a rough time last night." I just mumbled because was I delirious with exhaustion. "You gonna take the class at home?" He was talking about a Web-cast course I was scheduled for on micro-wave equipment. I don't understand why because we never touch the microwave equipment. Again in a mumbled voice I said, "Uh, yeah, just getting up and getting ready" which was a half-truth. I was up because I had set my alarm, but I was lying in bed debating on whether to blow it off because I worked to 6:00AM and just cat napped. I said I would be in.

I am writing this on a break. I keep dosing off and I hear the instructor calling, "Ed, are you there?" My head jerks up and I click on the acknowledge button.

In the interest of civility, I emailed my manager and requested if I could bill OT for the carrier add I worked last night or if he would prefer I'll take comp time or time off instead of the OT pay. I did this because I keep hearing about watching the OT. I'm trying to help him out, work with him be a team player? As usual, I get the ambiguous reply, "Code the time to carrier adds code." Like I didn't already know that? He doesn't tell me to enter the code as regular time or enter it as over time; you know I choose the overtime! Often he would reply to questions with a somewhat scripted and open ended response like "we have vehicles for that" or "our policy is not to reject tickets" and it all sounds ridiculous. I know he wasn't smart enough to come up with these replies on his own. They could just be answered simply "yes" or "no." or "do this" or "do that." I have to assume he was responding with some coached scripted management bullshit he learned in a seminar; in fact I took psych 101, I'm sure of it.

Wednesday, January 30, 1999 7:30AM

Got into last night about rejecting tickets with my manager. I rejected a ticket because I deemed it was unsafe travel duration: and it was! I put right in the ticket "Unobtainable and unsafe travel duration" and rejected it. Dispatch immediately called me "you can't do that! And I said "I just did!" I am just sick of these tickets piling up and being bullied to keep accepting them when everyone knows I can't get to them. Five minutes didn't go by and my manger calls and goes right into his scripted "we don't reject tickets,

*we don't reject tickets, we don't reject tickets... that's all he
kept repeating. I said "you know I can't get there, why I
would accept it when I have the option to reject it?" He would
just say "we don't reject tickets, we don't reject tickets" with
the occasional "if you have issues call me" I'm thinking why?
So you can read me your "we don't reject tickets" script. He
knows the problem is fudged travel durations that are
unobtainable as well we are way under manned. When I was
listening to him it reminded me of The Caine Mutiny, where
Humphery Bogert plays a Navy Captain who loses it on the
witness stand and starts babbling about "the strawberries...it
was the strawberries."*

I can't call him and tell him I am not going to accept a ticket
because of travel durations and he knows it. Hell he
probably set the ticket up. He is just hiding behind the
software and I'm just starting to get disgusted with it all and
decided to reject a ticket in frustration.

Below is an email to clarify working with CO (Central Office)
or switch techs and reporting problems to another support
team?

Team,

*There has been some discussion and confusion on who
calls the Support team. This should clear it up.*

*If you are working a joint ticket / Shared Task you are
obviously working with the switch tech at that time. If
after the two of you identify the problem being on site or
in the shelter, the Field Tech is to call into the Support
BRIDGE and report the problem.*

*If the switch tech has the time to call or report a problem,
then that is something for the 2 of you to work out. What
may not be known is that the Switch techs may be*

working with multiple field techs and/or working with
other teams on separate switch issues.

You see countless cases in this book where managers give vague answers, wrong answers, and my personal favorite: scripted answers which equal "no answer".

I think this entire manager/worker relationship would have been so much better if there was less management and more workers. Add to that a manager who is not too good to came out and ride in the truck once a month with a different underling, a manager would become an enlightened supervisor by experiencing how insane a typical shift operated. Not only would he have more empathy for his workers, but he could also take it to *his managers* and explain how some things need to be changed to be more productive.

This does not sound like rocket science to me. If a company were in business to make money, doing something along these lines to make work more efficient would enhance the bottom line. Maybe I am being too optimistic, but I think focusing on a better workflow, less chiefs and more Indians and making more money is not a bad idea!

Wednesday September 14, 2011

1:30AM - Another 13-hour day. Normally someone installs the equipment one day and I come by and perform the calibrations the next night. Now my manager has decided to have me do both installation and calibration in the same shift. I had better not hear a word about OT.

This particular model of equipment I have never calibrated before. As usual, it was a pain in the ass. First,

146

they were not sure if the LEC had even installed the new T1 circuit. This in of itself takes a couple hours to verify circuits to work orders with the switch operator (SO). Then I had to physically find it, test it, and verify it was the right circuit coming into the site from the road. Then I have to punch it down and test it back toward my equipment under the tower. Then test the whole circuit with the SO; all in the allotted time of 1.5 hours?

They are up my ass for this inventory bullshit. "Sarbanes Oxley" or "Sox" is a new law. Thanks to the fuck stains at Enron, corporations now have to report their inventory to the government so they can be taxed accordingly. I hope Ken Lay's (Google the name) heart attack lasted days, and he died a slow agonizing and painful death that cock sucker and I hope the rest of them got traded for cigarettes. The problem is I cannot transfer any parts within the inventory database because they have not been released by the prior market. So now I have to send emails requesting they be released and they'll want to know why and probably say I need manager approval. What crushes us is they think all this work should take two hours and inevitably, it takes all day.

12:45PM - *Getting ready to head in early to get a jump on things. I'm scheduled to start at 2PM but I desperately need to print some files and travel receipts but no one can access the printer at the shop because we're not allowed to plug in to the network. Here I am at this billion-dollar company and I do not have access to a networked printer. If I do not print a receipt report, I cannot get reimbursed for expenses, and the then I have to pay late fees on the credit card. Pretty slick of the company to put the travel card in our names. We get the money deposited in our accounts, like a paycheck and then we pay the credit card company. So if you think about it, they have taken the tax burden for "their"* *travel expenses and put it on me by increasing my taxable income! Could you at least kiss me?*

I ended up plugging my laptop straight into the USB port on the printer.

Chapter 14

Yin and Yang of a Typical Shift

Tuesday May 3, 2011

They killed Bin Laden yesterday; don't get me wrong, I wept openly on Sept, 11. And even went to a church service. But I can't help thinking how the narcissistic cock suckers on Wall Street whom caused this great recession and destroyed millions upon millions of lives, did far more damage to our country than Al Qaeda could have ever dreamed...

I added this entry because 2008 the great recession will go down in the annals of history how greed and narcissism dismantled the middle class of America. These are supposed to be educated men well versed in economic history. You know they all went to some zippy prep schools getting their "superior education?" I believe it was a financial coup d'état and if you agree with me then they are guilty of treason, and you know the penalty for that is? People have said "oh that's offensive" you can't say that, there was no loss of life." I thought about it. I have personally lost several close friends whom I attribute their death as a result of Wall Street wiping out their retirement and home equity and all hope of ever getting a well-paying job again. Could you imagine if they privatized Social Security as there was once talk of? And I don't care where the market is now it doesn't change the last 7 years. The year 2008 is still mentioned and as I write it is going on 2015. How many of you know someone or know of someone even now who is slowly killing themselves in some capacity because they have given up all hope; and if you think "well they didn't break any laws" that's because they are above the law which is fine! We don't have to waste time with a trial. I believe anyone or organizations with that kind of power is in complete contradiction to the idea of our democracy. Furthermore if I was responsible for the damage they caused to the masses I would have gone in the back yard and done the honorable thing and I am not alone in that thought. Google the name "Hiroo Tominaga" with "JAL" Of course these men have no honor its non-existent in a corporate board room or on Wall St, it cannot exist; it doesn't have a "margin" or a "metric?"...and speaking of honor. Even now you have kids sacrificing themselves on grenades for their fellow Americans while unregulated electronic traders are front running and high frequency trading on Wall St; along with the Bernie Madoff's, Bank and Health Ins oligarchs; all raping the wealth of our democracy with a sense of entitlement and the remorse of a tyrannical monarch?

Monday July 18 2011

I heard a commercial on the radio for a pawn shop. It said something about an "award for integrity" I thought to myself ..."who is running around awarding pawn shops for integrity?" Like the guy hawking his tools for crack is gonna take a cab across town to get to your pawn shop for the "integrity?" I thought it was funny...

Wednesday February 15, 2013

I pulled into a convenience store to grab a pack a nabs and coffee. As I park and immediately jump on my laptop and start IM'ing dispatch. It's the routine any time you stop you IM because it's obviously easier then when you drive. As I am sitting there someone pulls up on my passenger side. I can hear the thumpty, thump thump but I really don't pay it much attention.

My truck is my office and I needed to get some documentation. It was in my backpack on the passenger side floor. I cannot even come close to reaching it as I have a console with my laptop up and stacks of binders and tools in the passenger seat. So I jumped out and walked around and as I approached the car next to me I show my hands and gesture to my door. It's obviously too loud to say anything but I'm thinking this is the universal sign "hey I'm not a threat." I get a look of bewilderment. But I have my hands up and continue on doing my best to show "I'm really very busy and I could care less what you are doing, I just need to open my passenger door." Just as I get around and open my door I look at him again to say "it's cool" because of course we still couldn't speak. Well this guy jumps out and comes right at me. Call me a master of the obvious! But my SA (situational awareness) told me he didn't want to exchange greeting cards. Without hesitation I stand up and step right back at him and now we are standing inches apart. I think I said "WHATS YOUR FUCKING PROBLEM MOMMY DIDN'T CUT THE CRUSTS OFF YOUR SANDWICHES?" not that he even heard me; I think he called me a "cracker." After that who knows? We are inches apart just yelling at each other "fuck you!" And "fuck you too!", I was seriously considering kicking him in the balls. Then he leans back and feigns like he is reaching for something in his car and I didn't flinch. Oh I was watching his hands! I almost reached in my pack back and grabbed my 40 and said "LOOKING FOR ONE OF THESE!" He was bigger than me but I just kept watching his hands and stood my ground. I think that startled him too. By now people were starting to stop and look. I knew cameras are everywhere. I was in a company truck and if the cops showed up I would probably lose my job. I was shaking I was so pissed off. Again he called me a "cracker" and walked towards the store, really...a cracker?

Actually I'm a Pollock with a small dick...and I can't dance either. I stood there for about 30 seconds just stewing and debating whether to wait and go at it again or call my friends in the 1% motorcycle club that I was in as a "hang around." I show this guy a universal sign of peace and respect and he comes at me! Most of them were very "ethnocentric" (look it up!) to put it mildly and if they showed up this guy would have ended up in the lake...alive! I ended up jumping in my truck and speeding off. I had to get out of there quick as it would have escalated and I didn't want to end up in jail or on the evening news. As that doesn't look to good on your review. "Stereotypes...they come from reality"

As I read this let me reiterate where my heads at when I am at work. I have three cell phones two of which are constantly "dinging" away with voice mail notifications. I have my laptop which is up and constantly "pinging" at me with IM's from dispatch and emails from who knows? I have a personal laptop as well. I have a laptop login, windows login, an aircard login, I have a VPN login, just to get to my ticketing app login with tickets piling up and the myriad of database apps that I need and ALL of them are always dropping as I drive around. I have two GPS systems yelling at me with directions; one in a sexy English voice for some much needed humor. I say this to drive home the fact how far removed I am from someone who I can only surmise wants to listen to loud music and bongo's to celebrate their ethnicity: and yet is still very angry about it? I really don't care. I am busy trying to defy the laws of physics so I can keep my job and by that I mean I have been forced to accept a ticket that's says I will be on a site 60 miles away in one half hour.

Wednesday August 21 2013 7:15AM

Came up on a bad accident tonight. I was driving along and my window is down as it's a nice summer night. I am on a major throughway in town and as I slow down to a red light

I hear yelling. I look over to my left across the intersection I see someone lying in the road and people yelling and running towards the scene. Obviously this had just happened. I heard someone yell the car that hit this person just took off. I yelled out "which way and what was it!" They yelled" it was a brown 4 door and it went that way!" that's all I heard. I hit my cherry top flashers cut a U-turn running the red light and took off. I went flying down the road as fast as I could but I didn't see anything in front of me. I came up on a red light so that was as much as I could do. I turned around and headed back to the scene. I came up on the same light and as I looked over this time I saw a scooter up on the sidewalk near a telephone pole. It was around midnight so fortunately there was not much traffic but I could see cars at the next intersection down the road getting ready to come this way. What concerned me was with a green light here they would just blow right through running someone over. I pulled across the intersection and parked my truck in the oncoming lane at an angle to block traffic. Obviously with my cherry top flashers and waited for the emergency services. I heard someone say "he said he can't move his legs!" It was eerie because I could see he was lying on his stomach and the tops of his feet were flat on the ground. That image is ingrained in my mind and I cringe at the thought because I ride a motorcycle. I'm sure he was paralyzed. It wasn't long the cops showed up. I said "I didn't see it happen but I didn't want to see the poor guy get run over again!" He said "no problem thanks for the help." I took off and went back to work.

Maybe some Karma?

Tuesday May 21, 2013

I had a ticket for a T1 circuit down and when I opened the shelter and stepped inside some dude was lying on the floor in a sleeping bag. I woke him up when he heard me come in. Believe it or not I wasn't really startled. I am surprised it doesn't happen more often. Nothing surprises me anymore. That's what I like about the job in the first place. I said "hey man what's up?" He said "oh, hey, I just came up from Louisiana and I'm working on something" I forget what. I said "no biggie, saving on some per diem eh?" he said "yea I sure am." I know no one is going to get in these shelters if they don't belong. They are fully enclosed no windows. You have to have a key or combo; they are very secure. We chatted briefly, by his knowledge and demeanor I wasn't even remotely concerned. He went back to sleep and I reset some equipment to clear alarms and I left; just another day in the life.

I guarantee if I raised a stink and called my manager eventually we would find out he was supposed to be there. I'm sure he was a sub of a sub of sub of sub...in fact I know it! Mean while my tickets would be piling up and I guarantee I would have wasted a whole day trying to find the department that out sourced this guy and then get an email from my manager a week later about ticket backlogs and why I didn't get anything done today; see the beauty of outsourcing?

Friday July 1st 2013 6:40AM

I was in Winston-Salam last night in a sort of sketchy part of town. Although having been to Newark and the lower east side of Manhattan growing up its debatable? I had just

finished installing a modem card and was sitting in my truck outside the gate closing out my ticket. I have my cherry-top flashers going as always cause it scares away possible trouble. Well that's the idea anyways. I'm sitting there knee deep in my laptop and I hear a tap on my window. It startled me. I look up and I see a Blond girl. I immediately look to my passenger side mirror to make sure no one is coming up my side and I'm not being set up to be robbed. I turn back, crack my window and say "hey what's up?"She says "hi you doing ok?" I said "yeah I'm fine, busy as usual what are you doing?" Not like I meant it. She said "I was just at the bar across the street and I saw you sitting here and..." I cut her off and in a short tone bluntly said "yeah I saw all the cars...I'm just working", basically saying I'm very busy and I don't have time for this shit. She caught on and said "ok sorry to bother you, good night." I said "bye" and dove back into my laptop looking at the ticket I just received while talking to her. I kept glancing at my passenger side mirror for precaution. After about 5 minutes I pulled out and as I drove down the street I saw her standing in a dimly light store entrance and as she waved I had an "AH HA moment!"
...She was a prostitute.

Friday February 3, 2012 7:30AM

Holy shit! Talk about a WTF moment! It was around 3AM I was parked outside a tower in the middle of a field in total Zen with my laptop completely absorbed in my part ordering databases and trouble tickets and KA-BAM! My whole truck shakes like I got hit. And I did! A herd of cows had surrounded me and one was rubbing up against my truck. There was a huge eyeball in the cargo window behind my seat..."attack of the mutant eyeballs"..lol!, scared the shit out of me...

Saturday October 27, 2012 8:20PM

I pulled over and stopped in a small strip mall parking lot to do some admin. Check trouble tickets, IM dispatch, look at some emails and get ready for my next site. While I'm working I glance up and see what looks like an attractive woman walking up the side walk. I'm in the middle the parking lot so she is about a hundred feet away? She was a brunette in tight jeans wearing some sexy boots and sunglasses. She looked good! I went back to work knee deep in my laptop and applications. After a couple of minutes I happened to glance up and she had stopped and was waving in my direction? I looked around didn't see any other cars so I sort of waved back...not really sure if she was waving at me? When I did she started towards me. I immediately checked my passenger side mirror and looked around make sure nothing fishy was going on. I then thought hmm, maybe this is someone who needs a hand. It wasn't a few weeks ago I pumped an elderly woman's gas because she was having trouble with the pump. Things happen although I am always leery. As she approached I stuck my head out the window and she said "can you give me a lift up the road?" I said "yeah if it's not too far." She said "it's the HD shop up the street." Like I haven't been there a hundred times? I said "com'on, get in." As she climbed in I could see she was a little tweaked on something but still she didn't look to bad and I was heading that way anyways. As we drove she said something about her friend in a motel room. So now I am thinking "ah ha! Gotta live one here!"... I said "what's going on at the HD shop?"After about 10 seconds of awkward silence she looked straight at me and said "200 dollars!" Without hesitation I said "100!" and then I said "let's go there's a cell site shelter right up the road." I was laughing to myself because I'm thinking "do it in a shelter so she could

156

be like a metaphor for management". She said she was staying...or working at the Hampton Inn near where I was parked. I said "that's OK, but I will tell you right now I'm bringing my 40 so don't have someone waiting for me" and reached into my tool bag on the back seat. "She said oh no, no, I'm not like that." And to be honest I believed her. We talked for a bit and I even took her to lunch. I have heard her story from people all over the country. It always starts out with "when the economy went bad" Turned out she lived nearby and even knew a buddy of mine. I'm a pretty good read on people so I wasn't too worried about getting rolled. Still I ended up taking my 40 and laid it on the bed stand. It was like an erotic scene in a gangster movie and I thought it was cool. There is an old expression. "Treat and lady like a whore and a whore like a lady."

Sorry if this offends anyone but the way I see it as a man, one way or the other we all pay for it. Some women are just less subtle about it, or honest, depending on how you look at it. And let me postscript this by saying it's no coincidence the main character in "Fifty Lamp Shades of off White" is a billionaire. In the movie trailer could you imagine if he shows her his smut room and then said "If you want to leave I have to wait for my mother to get home to borrow her car," he would be a creep! But because he blurts out "I have a helicopter!" *like what's he gonna do, drop her off at a strange airport?* That is supposed to instantly justify it and make it all acceptable, hmm... why is that? I'm sorry but the insinuation is not very flattering ladies and if I was woman I would be insulated.

Besides every book has to have some salacious sex and this is mine. With regards to the job by now I really didn't give a shit anymore. I had just gotten into another shouting match with my manager. I just didn't care, I was a broken man.

Monday March 19, 2012 6:40AM

I was working a calibration last night on a site a good half mile if not more back off a dead end road. On the way I passed a few homes but it was pretty remote. It's about 2AM and I was in the middle of calibrating when I heard a real loud yelping or yelling. I don't know how to describe it but whatever it was...it was manmade. Someone was in the woods just beyond the fence trying to fuck with me. As I have said before when I am on the job it's pretty intense. Even at 2AM my laptops dinging away with dispatch bullying me into accepting even more tickets. It might as well be 2PM. I have a test set that weighs 40lbs and my laptop logged in controlling the entire site with a vendor app that is flakey to say the least. I'm climbing all over the platform connecting and reconnecting cables, co-ax and cat5, and hard lines that run up the tower, loading amplifiers and I/O cards, tools are everywhere, I'm looking at manuals and documentation, realigning lights so I can see what I'm doing...its hard work and hectic! So when I heard this noise by someone trying to fuck with me I was really more annoyed and pissed off then scared.

I reached in my tool bag and pulled out my 40. I purposely held it up high above the hum of the equipment and chambered a round with the infamous CLICK-CLACK! Making sure they would hear it. Needless to say whatever it was it went silent. I listened intently for someone running away but I never heard it. I thought about firing off a round but I waited and never heard it again. After about 5 minutes I went back to work with my SA (situational awareness) turned up all the way , "it goes to 11" I finished the calibration now I am home.

Maybe it was a lawyer making sure my TRACK logo was taped over? Seriously, when I read this it aggravates me that I was out there by myself. Despite thinking I'm a badass there really should be two man teams for safety and this is a perfect example. If a couple of people wanted to roll me they probably could. One of the guys I work with said he knew of a guy that got stabbed. If management knew I had a gun they would fire me on the spot. Yet! They constantly send me out to potentially dangerous situations with no regard for my well being. That's why we had to carry. A lot of the techs did. Reminds me of what a cop once told me when I was in the back of his car after a bar room brawl which I did not start and I didn't! He said "better to be judged by twelve then carried by six" yes sir!

Sunday December 23, 2012 7:40PM

It is Sunday two days before Christmas but as usual I worked all day. It's funny but when I first started out of college businesses would shut down the whole week between x-mas and new year's, it was a given. I lost another good friend today. Can't say I'm totally shocked. Not sure what to think, just numb? I got a phone call from a mutual friend this afternoon. He went to his first wife's grave and shot himself.

He had contacted me a few months ago. I received an email that said "I need to disappear." I remember that struck me as an odd thing to say. I replied "can I relate, me too what's up?" He was in Florida and I told him to come on up to NC if he needs to get away.

I met him years ago riding motorcycles. He was in computer sales and like most of us in the nineties he was doing well. He had a beautiful wife and nice home on a golf course. He was a Navy vet who grew up in Boston. A beer drinking, bar brawling Italian Jew, who looked like Vin Diesel and one of the funniest people I ever met.

Quick anecdote: We were in a bar at Myrtle Beach during bike week. He was very charismatic and had no problem with the ladies. Well some guy got a little jealous and they started to exchange words. Just as they squared off my buddy whack's himself on the side of the head and raises his fists. The whole place went silent. I looked at the guy he was to about fight and he looked at me. We both had expressions of pure bewilderment: like "did he really just slap himself on the side of head?" I quickly seized the comical moment and whisked by buddy out the door. He didn't even realize what he did...it was classic!

When I met him he had beautiful baby girl with his first wife. Tragically his wife would die of brain cancer not long after. Now he was with his second wife with whom he had three more daughters. I guess you could call it Karma? She had filed for divorce and taken all four daughters out west with her new boy friend. Don't get me wrong my friend was no angel by any stretch but like a lot of us he lost everything.

Now he was out of work and broke bouncing between my couch and his cousins. He wanted to sell me his motorcycle so he had some money to travel. I figured he was going to his girlfriends in Ohio. I gave him $5000 for the bike with the intention of selling it. He also persuaded me to throw in my HK-40 as he was going to be out on the road. I thought "yeah when I travel I like to pack too." Plus I felt a little guilty for only giving him 5k for the bike.

He left and went to Ohio but within a week he came right back. After that he sat around drinking every day. He told me he had pancreatic cancer on numerous occasions. He looked pretty gaunt but I don't know? He kept saying "I'm tired, I'm tired" and "I'm worth more dead, I'm worth more dead" speaking about his children. We talked of two of our mutual friends who on separate occasions had committed suicide a few years ago. They had lost it all too. It may seem morbid but one time he said "I'm gonna haunt you!" and we laughed out loud and I said "tell Dave and Tony I said hi!" Another time I got angry and called his bluff. I said "go ahead then just fucking do it! Get it over with!" My thinking was he just wanted to convince someone that was all. Keep in mind I'm still working 16 hours a day so I'm exhausted and in my own hell.

Sometimes it really fucks with me and then I have to realize it's what he wanted and no one could have stopped him. He spoke of it like he was planning a trip and in retrospect sometimes I don't have a problem with it. It may sound callous but it's a way to take control of the uncontrollable. I believe the sanctity of my life can only come from within and not from some stranger trying to impose their religious agenda under the guise of "concern." If I chose to end it then I want my decision to be respected and that was pretty much what he conveyed to me. He was tired and had had enough.

Different circumstances similar notion is the young woman named Brittany Maynard who was just in the news for physician assisted suicide. Without question an epic tragedy but to me she is a saint and a hero. She said "fuck you cancer, I'm taking control of the situation." God bless her! Talk about courage! If you were faced with her situation could you do it? Don't get me wrong I would like to stick around for a while and plan on it. But we are all born and we all die. In English Lit we studied a famous poem by John Donne titled: *"Death, be not proud"*…the title says it all.

"History is made up of thousands of lives." ~ LCPL Jessie Strong, KIA Jan. 26 2005 –Iraq

161

Thursday January 3 2013 2:40AM

Had a funny experience tonight; I pulled in to a convenience store to get a coffee about an hour ago. The place was lit up like a Christmas tree so I knew it was open. I jump out of the truck and in my usual Olympic paced walk, trot up and yank on the door. I heard a faint "click" but it didn't register. My hand slips off the handle and I almost go flying on my ass. I gather myself and yank again...it's locked! I peer through the door and give the clerk the look of "dude...WTF?" He was looking back at me with eyes as big as manhole covers pointing to his head. It took a second to sink in. I had my hoodie up. I flipped it back smiled and laughed. He did the same, buzzed the door and let me in. I walked in laughing "sorry man, thought I was gonna rob you eh!" He said "yeah I saw you coming up to the door" I said I'm from up north, if you walk slow you get run over. He has a button he can push to lock the door if he thinks someone suspicious is coming in. I called it his "panic button" and said "to bad the walkway doesn't drop out too" He laughed. I said "I need one those for when my boss calls me". We joked some more and I apologized again and told him my work has sucked the ability to think about anything else right out of me.

Friday August 26, 2011

I was driving up the highway 40 today and I have a left lane exit. It's in the middle of Greensboro NC right where Interstates 85 and 40 merge together. You have to get over and off in the left lane for this particular exit. Well I get in the left lane because I have to and some car is right on my ass. I'm pretty sure he doesn't realize there's an exit coming up and nor do I like being in the left lane only doing the speed limit. I can see this clown in my rear mirror yelling and *freaking out. I exit off and as he drives by on the right I see his arm fly out the window with his middle finger in the air. His license plate says New Jersey...I laughed out loud!*

Chapter 15

Without Your Health, You Have Nothing

Wednesday November 9, 2011

Gotta email about our health ins apparently Verizon techs ? are on strike for medical benefits something to that effect? So to one up SWEDEN announced 100% coverage as of the first of the year.

Don't get me wrong this is a great benefit. Still I am suspicious as nothing is free and while I don't want to seem un-grateful I'm thinking *"so what! I'm working 80 + hours a week so I'm really still paying for it"* I'm sure some exec said "sure, just make sure they work the extra hours to cover our costs." So now I'll be working 90 hours and week. Besides I don't think it's really a benefit, it's all been calculated in some "algorithms" or "process" to get twice the work out of one employee.

Monday June 18, 2012

Gotta tattoo, just tried to do a job on Ft. Bragg. After an hour and half drive, which was the allotted time for the whole ticket; then going through base security, then driving all over to find the building and then making phone calls for an hour only to find out I can't get roof top access to the equipment. No one is available to let me on the roof, hell no one even knows who the POC is anymore the name listed in the site database has been gone for years. Now I'm stuck with the ticket which will just get pushed further and further out as more pile up. Eventually it will show up on some report and I will get a email from my manager stating that he got chewed out over a ticket that never got "resolved" I will tell him what happened and he'll say "call so and so or see what you can do" Like I have the time for that? If I just blow it off and close the ticket with some made up bull shit then I get a call about tickets being closed and the site is still having the same trouble. It's like the harder I try the more I fail…

I am just so beaten down, exhausted, worn out, and depressed, angry, I am empty from the continual harassment with tickets that just keep piling up knowing I'll never get to them I can't fix them and I am becoming despondent. Bing more tickets! YOU WILL ACCEPT! PING! More tickets YOU WILL ACCEPT…BING! BING! BING! ACCEPT THIS TICKET..YOU WILL ACCEPT THIS TICKET!..is this the rest of my life, and all for what? That's what I can't wrap my head around. I am numb and there is nothing I can do about it so I wanted to try and feel. I wanted to get "PAIN" tattooed on my knuckles but that's fairly common. I got to thinking and I decided to put a spin on it. I got "PANE" because I'm in it and I see it everywhere I go, everywhere I have been and everywhere I look. I was driving through Fayetteville typical military town, pawn shops, tattoo parlors and dry cleaners. I walked in a tat shop and told the girl "drill me, hard! 'P'-'A'- 'N'- 'E'… on all four knuckles, right on the bone…hurt me! I dare you!"

I didn't feel a thing.

Wednesday July 13, 2011 4:40PM

Just woke up. I had to take some meds to help me sleep this morning. I was exhausted. I have terrible panic attacks. When I keep pushing myself to stay up, it becomes like a runaway train. I cannot go to sleep, and not being able to fall asleep turns into panic because work is looming and I worry how I will function or drive if I do not sleep. Then I cannot go to work, or worse there is no one to do it and it will pile up on me. I just felt a twinge in my chest. It's nothing...but what if it's not? My palms are sweaty...oh its nothing...but what if it's not...Oh it's just in your head...but what if it's not. I don't want to be alone what if something happens to me! Will they'll find my body on the floor, maybe this time it's a real heart attack! Oh its nothing...but it's hard to breath; my chest is tight, why! Its happens ...sometimes they find people days later. Maybe this is really it, its really my time. Oh it's just in your head...but what if it's not!. Maybe it's really gonna happen this time...and I'm all alone...

A panic attack is just debilitating not to mention the scariest thing I have ever experienced; I wouldn't wish it on anyone. It's like a runaway train and just the thought of one can trigger it. That's how fucked up it is and people who have had one know exactly what I am talking about.

Email: Urgent Action: Message sent with High Importance. I am sitting here thinking of this Work Force Management (WFM) software which is how we get our tickets. It is supposed to "automate the workforce" which if you think about it conceptually means that I am working for software or machines. Talk about Orwellian: kind of scary.

Besides sharing with you some of the general BS I typically put up with, what I want to highlight by the entries in this chapter is the very real affect work had on my health. And it was not just me, it happened to so many of us. Everyone I worked with was on anxiety and sleeping meds including me. I think you have a flavor of my typical shifts: long hours, long drives, and a lot of stress being told "put this round peg in a square hole and you have one hour to drive sixty miles and back to complete it or we're calling your mother!"

Somewhere in the recent history of corporate America, we went from a work ethic that was unrivalled to pushing people beyond endurance. Stress and overwork are terms commonly heard in the business world. Even though some people believe that stress helps them work better and working lots of hours is great, it is actually damaging to both your health and your business. For some insane reason, it became a badge of honor about how many hours a person could work. In some corporate circles, it became the equivalent of seeing whose penis is bigger. The result is people being utterly stupid and in my line work dangerous and for what?

According to a number of recent studies, approximately half of all employed people feel that they face overworking issues, to the point where they are not as healthy as they could be. Health impacts related to overworking issues include headaches, fatigue, extreme tiredness, regular sleepiness, continuous irritability, and even panic attacks.

Like most people, I like to think I am unique. The truth is that this is exactly what I experienced. God forbid if you actually bitch to management about the time you were putting in to the job. The truth is that people who believe that they are suffering from overworking issues are not simply whining. In fact, the majority of people who feel that they are overworked, also claim that they do enjoy the challenges presented at their jobs (like me), and many claim to feel more fulfilled when they are busy than when they are more idle.

However, even when a person enjoys his or her work, and feels fulfilled by being busy, the fact is that overworking issues must be taken very seriously due to their risk of causing work-related illnesses, a growing resentment about the long hours and sensations of losing control over their life. These overworking issues will only continue, and possibly grow, as the workload experienced by employees continues to rise. As I allude to in my forward I see it as form of capitalism consuming us.

I understand there will be some stress at work; that's why it is called "work"; I get it! But after eight hours of intense troubleshooting and maintenance on complex cellular networks you encounter what Economists call "the law of diminishing returns." I believe the solution to overworking issues is as simple as observing the prescribed eight hour work day or shift. The eight-hour day is not a revolutionary idea...although on second thought maybe it is? It requires an entire reworking of many of the attitudes within the workplace. The problem is that the management philosophy I ran into was to treat people like they were; quantified mouse clicks in some application. Personally I found it to be disrespectful not only to me but to my family and friends. I really believe the only thing that would have made my company wake up to the problem is if we had a union to force them to make some changes.

I would think from a management perspective unions would be an asset in that labor becomes a fixed cost? Holy shit! You might even create a sense of pride in the work place. As you may have gathered by now, a few simple remedies would have contributed to a much more efficient situation with some moral too. Or as we used to say "the beatings will stop as soon as they are assigned a code."

Thursday September 13, 2012

I had to drive to Florida and stage for a hurricane yesterday. Thank god they didn't need us and sent us right back. The ride was hell. Initially I had no idea what was going down there or behind or under me and by that I mean my ass! I recently hit the mile stone of 50. Jokingly I would say "I made to 50 I won!" I think father time in an effort to remind me whose boss gave me a hemorrhoid, yippee!

I don't know how to describe it, I have never had one but it really started burning and itching. Just like the commercials I was miserable or I am sure woman who have had kids can relate as apparently they are common with pregnancy? When I returned from Florida I finally figured it out. I'm the proud owner of a hemorrhoid. I should give it a name!

You should have seen me in the bathroom waddling around with a mirror between my legs trying to see it. I was laughing out loud when I wasn't wincing with soreness. It looked like a piece of broccoli sticking out of my asshole. When I went to the doctor's office it was full of older people; the ones that made it to over time in the game of life; all gingerly walking around with an obvious expression of discomfort. So when I go in to see the doc he tells me to drop my pants climb on his examination table and lay on my side. Of course he has a pretty young nurse assisting him. I am completely stripped of my dignity but looking for some humor in the situation I told him I had just turned 50 and this was my gift. He asked if I lift weights and I told him leg presses I'm too old to squat. He said it's not uncommon to see guys like me. I was pleasantly surprised when he asked me if I wanted him to "cut it off." I said "hell yeah!" and then I asked him if I could keep it to show off to my friends? He said "we don't do that." I was kidding...well sort of? On the way home I saw a bill board "Hemorrhoids" and it occurred to me all the commercials I see on TV. Apparently they are big business?

Since this chapter is about health I figured I would add this excerpt. My friend's wife told me to start eating prunes. Naturally (no pun intended) this lasted about two weeks. For the record this is in no way an insinuation that it was work related. When life gives you hemorrhoids, give them a name, the laughs on me!

Saturday September 10, 2011 8:00AM

I slept for 16 hours, and man do I feel great!

Thursday September 8, 2011

9:20AM - Thank God it was really slow and I didn't have to do any calibrations. I could not get to sleep so I took a Xanax and then my buddy's girlfriend called me in tears because they just broke up. After speaking with her, I was all spun up, so I took another Xanax because I had to get to sleep.

I woke up at 8:30PM to my alarm in a total fog. I did not see any tickets for the scheduled calibration but then panic! Maybe the ticketing app is AFU (all fucked up) again. I called my manager and said, "Hey, what's up with the calibration?" He said they cancelled it. I was so relieved because I was exhausted and they always turn into 11 and 12 hour jobs.

I woke up at midnight. I called dispatch and when I was on the phone I said, "If you have anything in Charlotte let me know. I'll take a look, but I am not making any promises." Sure enough, I ended up in Charlotte and when I got back home. I received another ticket for Charlotte. It was low priority and an hour and half away. I called dispatch and said, "I respectfully decline, that is not my market." That is when she got all pissy and said, "We don't work like that around here. Who is your manager?" So I told her. My manager called me five minutes later and said I had to go back. He said since I was "on-call" I had to go. Needless to say, I was pissed. I am just physically drained.

Many people take overwork very lightly and see it as "the more hours you work the better it is for the business" when in fact, studies have shown that the first 40 hours a week are worth much more to the company than the next 20 or 30 thirty extra hours. Believe me, there were many weeks where I became "counter-productive" because I put in many of those extra hours. Often as I would get into ten twelve, sixteen hours in to my shift I would start to question "why" what is this all for? I served in the Marine Corps I know what it's like to be pushed to your limits but this time I' am not fighting to save the free world! I'm just putting money in some ones pocket and I am ok with that to an extent. But now I m fighting exhaustion which metaphorically turns into a fight with management and the greedy mother fuckers who refuse to adhere to the long recognized eight hour shift;"why!" At what point does capitalism become tyrannical? In my mind I'm killing myself all because some zip doesn't have the balls to go home and tell his wife she has enough shoes. Then I start to think! What about all the people still unemployed looking for work thanks to the great recession? And here I am sometimes working 24 hours in a single shift; W.T.F.? The coup de grace is when I look at the calendar and it's the year 2011? I think you understand it perpetuates all the stress with the anger. Can you say "medication?"

Sleep or rest is just as important as food and sex. You have to have it to recharge your batteries and function as normal person. Then you can return to work feeling inspired to put more money in someone's pocket.

Like with so many issues, it starts at the top. When you have executives of the company arriving at the office at 6am and leaving at 9pm, it sends a signal to other employees that this is what is acceptable and expected when it most definitely should not be. Just because those executives, managers or fellow co-workers do not have a life or from what I have seen and heard just did not want to go home to their miserable marriage does not mean everybody should act that way. I for one like to go to the gym or visit my mother, watch Monday night football. You know! Enjoy "life" in the 21st century? Working too much can pose many stress-related health risks as well as damage personal relationships outside of work. I recall my manager openly stated his wife was leaving him because of the job. And let me add *"sympathy can be found between shit and syphilis in the dictionary"*

It has also been proven that working too many hours increases the possibilities of screwing up your job. However the greatest risk to us and "you"...was to drive with little to no sleep. We had to be in violation of DOT regulations. I think this is why they made us drive 1/4 ton trucks so DOT rules would not be applicable. We had a tech run a red light once and t-bone a car. He told me he was half asleep and the company with held the fact he had been working well in excess of 20 hours on that shift. We were always told an accident especially if it was your fault was grounds for immediate termination. Yet they did not fire him and I suspect if they did it would have been interrupted as an admission of guilt by corporate as well as an invitation to be investigated for violation of DOT and labor laws. You get the idea, though. Errors made by anyone due to overwork can be major and difficult to clean up; and again it's all for what?

Tuesday November 1, 2011

Gotta email bulletin from HR promoting health and well being...the importance to make time to "exercise" and diet! You know work/life balance?

Aaah! REALLY! Who the fuck sends stuff like this out? This is a real kick in the nuts for me. My biggest complaint is not having time to go to the gym. I lift and exercise religiously and work out despite management's efforts to thwart me. Even after 12 hour shifts I will try and find the energy to get to the gym. The point is exercise is important, its right there with food, sleep and sex. It infuriates me to no end they refuse to give us the time and then to send an email like this!

Stress causes terrible damage that can be both physical and mental. Even if you think your stressful work environment helps you get everything done, you might need to think about your health for a moment. People who experience chronic stress are more likely to develop stomach problems, sleep problems, heart disease, depression, obesity, substance abuse. Heck, I remember guys in boot camp who didn't have a blemish on arrival became almost unrecognizable from all the acne do to stress.

Your body cannot distinguish between physical and psychological threats, so if you are stressed over your busy work schedule your body is going to react in some capacity. In many cases, stress seems to sneak up on people and sink in so slowly that you might not even notice until one day you break down. The breakdown response could be in an agitated, depressed, or a tense frozen response. There are documented cases of stress leading to things like a stroke or heart attack and work place shootings. Which are becoming more common? Your stress levels may not be causing you any physical harm yet, but if it builds up enough, it definitely

173

will. I personally have lost several close friends to a heart attack and suicides; yes multiple. Two of them worked in the industry: one for AT&T and the other at Cisco. I attribute both of their deaths to being work related and others not being able to find it.

Thursday September 15, 2011

It's been three days since I have had a shower and I don't even care. These hours are starting to affect my health, I just shave my pits so I don't stink.

10:20AM *- I just woke up and all I'm thinking about is work. I kept dreaming about this Workforce Software. I left my phone in the truck last night and I am having anxiety about going to get it. I forgot to resolve the calibration ticket and to be honest, I do not care.*

Does the AWFS software know the company values and code of ethics? I wonder if those are integrated or written into the software, part of the "networked society" I keep hearing about?

Obviously, this was not a very good day. It was not uncommon to go days without a shower. Just walk in my apartment flip up my laptop for more work and pass out on the couch. A lot of my attitude can be attributed to a deep down in the bones weariness. It is like somewhere along the way the long hours, screwy procedures, and general bullshit broke my spirit. As you may have gathered, I always felt it was part of my teamwork mentality to do what was asked of me and put in the extra time. I'm a hard working Pollock from Jersey as well as ex-Marine; I always took pride in that. While hard work and long hours can certainly pay off, after a certain point, the quality of work diminishes, taking a heavy mental, emotional and physical toll. Eventually, it can diminish the quality of life.

Wednesday February 29,2012 4:00AM

Had a 24 hour shift on a two carrier adds. A calibration and line sweeps. I am sooo tried. I received a RF burn. I was removing the hard-line or co-ax and my hand went right over what's called a duplexer. It's what shoots the RF signal up and out the tower antennas. Don't get me wrong it's not like your skin melts away. If you get a finger or your hand to close it will burn you. It's the same concept as a laser only it's RF (radio frequency) not as far up on the electromagnetic spectrum. You don't even realize it at first then you feel a little burn or tingle. It itches for days. That's how you know you got one.

There is real truth to the saying, "All work and no play makes Jack a dull boy." Simply put, without a break from work, people become bored and boring because they have no outside interests. Work should be a means to an end, not the end in itself.

I know if I said any of this to a manager, he would call me a malcontent and that I did not know what I was talking about; "you're the only one having these issues." However, countless experiments over the years have proven that working too many hours decreases productivity. You are wearing yourself down emotionally and physically, and increasing the chances of burning out. Equally important is consistently working long hours also leads to sleep deprivation, which produces symptoms comparable to being legally drunk. Hell I remember having two days off in the month of October and that was because I just refused to work those two days. Again I keep asking myself for what?

Today, however, there are new reasons for working long hours. Thanks to technology, not only are you furthering your career and building a solid nest egg. Neat and sophisticated gadgets have made it painless. With your laptop, cell phone, PDA and GPS tracking and now Google glass you can be available and on the job 24/7. You can work straight until your retirement; never miss a day! I used to tell people "if I was anymore connected I would be the Matrix." hence the title of my book.

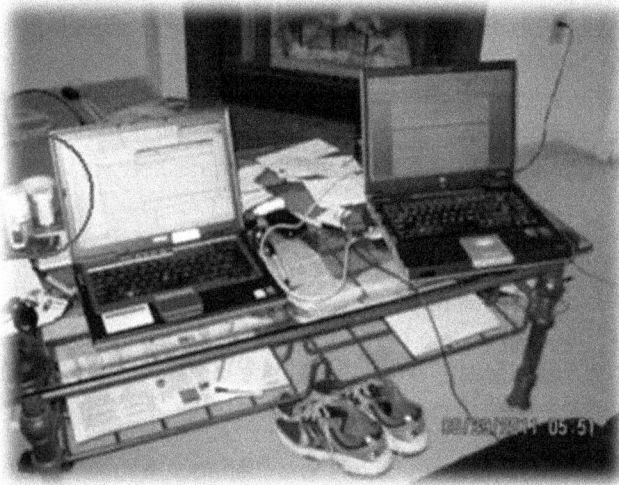

The grind and how I kept my journal. Come home boot up laptops, admin bullshit on work laptop left and journal entries on personal laptop on the right. Think to myself "self! You need to take a shower it's been 3 days" and pass out. Note meds center left.

While Ford took credit for the 40-hour workweek, he was not the first to come to the conclusion that it was worthwhile. Throughout the 30s, 40s and 50s, there were hundreds of studies praising the benefits of the 40-hour week and it's no coincidence this is when America really emerged as the premier super power?

If you are in a job abusing your physical and mental state, take stock. To quote Clint Eastwood in one of the *Dirty Harry* movies, "A man has to know his limitations."

Working smart means understanding these limits. You are no good to anyone, least of all yourself, if you are not in good mental and physical condition. Doctors and fitness experts constantly preach the importance of leading a balanced life. This means family, healthy eating, doing fun things and getting rest. Most importantly, not being pushed by your place of work into senseless extremes by executives and managers who have a confused notion they are on some great crusade; leading you into battle to rescue the new young receptionist...I mean fair maiden? Remember that old saying: "no one ever lied on their deathbed wishing they worked more" I doubt you are going to regret the extra time you could have spent at work."

Chapter 16

You Cannot Make This Stuff Up

Monday May 23, 2011

It's a Monday so the myriad of emails have started flying or I should say more than the usual. I have to submit my time for last week. Last Monday was a Floating Holiday and I keep getting errors when trying all the different codes. After an hour I finally call my manager who states, "Oh! There are no codes for time off!"

Friday June 17, 2011

I have a TRACK email and an SWEDEN email. We primarily use our TRACK accounts. I took a PTO (Personal Time Off) today and I need to check my SWEDEN email. It has been almost two weeks but that gives you an idea of how immersed I am in TRACK. Here is an email that is going around. Read it and draw your own conclusions.

"Urgent issue regarding SWEDEN laptops in TRACK buildings. Team: We need your immediate help to address an urgent issue. Based on the Customer Network Service contract, it is a violation to plug any laptop into TRACK's network using a cable. This applies to all areas in TRACK buildings, including office cubes or conference rooms. If you currently have an SWEDEN laptop and it is connected to TRACK's network using a cable, please disconnect it immediately. Contact your manager with questions or concerns."

Can someone explain how we are to support the customer if we cannot plug in to their network or how we are supposed to print? See title of chapter!

You know what this reminds of? The Cold War when the United States and the old Soviet Union played "keep away" from each other on everything from nuclear technology to the best tasting coffee. We were waging a very peculiar war with each other. Except back then, they were still able to come up with the technology so that an American Apollo spacecraft could link up with a Soviet Soyuz ship as a symbol of peace in outer space. However, I am not allowed to use my equipment to fix a customer's problem or print my package slips so I can get replacement parts because of some policy. Yet still make SLA's?

Monday August 29,2011 4:00PM

Email from manager about codes:

Ed,

Please remove the Network Coding from your ON-Call time sheet, On-Call does not get networking coding, But Call-IN does.

Have you ever noticed every now then you will catch a commercial that openly mocks the corporate culture? My favorite is "in order to achieve success I must portray success" while the guy is sitting in his garage that is decorated to look like a high end corner office; no coincidence it is a 'corner' office too! And then his wife opens the garage door and she even burns him about it; it's funny. A friend of mine, who happened to be in corporate hell and on meds, tried to defend it by sheepishly stating, "Well, perception is reality," to which I replied "That's exactly the idea Mephistopheles sold to Faustus, and he worked for the devil. It's what all the charlatan's preach on CNBC."

Looking back over the years, that was where I had the greatest difficulty, having to constantly deal with people trying to create their own reality because they did not want to deal with the one we were in. It's no wonder everyone in the corporate world is on anti-depressants and in therapy. I just couldn't do it, I refused...to go to therapy and I put the question to you. "How do you deal with someone who insists on creating their own reality?" I'm gonna call it/you out, not to be an asshole but I believe it is the right thing to do. You are not helping someone by pretending with them. To me that's my version of hell and what inspired me to keep a journal. Come to think of it... is probably why so many people in Hollywood are AFU, they are all walking around "pretending?" Going through my journal is not as much of a stroll down memory lane as it is a walk through the Twilight Zone and my English Literature course.

"Why this is hell, nor am I out of it." ~ **Mephistopheles**

Thursday June 23, 2011 8:00AM

I received a package in the mail today. I opened it and it's a plastic head with a DVD on how to perform CPR? Which of course I'm supposed to watch on my own time? I can guarantee you the company is now promoting us (field techs) as CPR qualified to meet some OSHA standard or something? I'm now CPR qualified...so if you are a mannequin working in the mall and you have a heart attack, you can rest easy, I will save you?

In my forward I mention how a union would being some pragmatism and this is good example. A company that is built on a growing mountain of bull shit is just going to sink under its own weight back into the manure...or a nation for that matter?

I know in parts of this book I push for ideas such as unions are needed in business again. One of the over-arching themes, though, is just how incompetent our multi-billion dollar industries can be. How some of these companies continue to earn huge stock increases is beyond me. I guess it just proves that how a company operates and its value on the Dow Jones is just a rigged price

The sad part that comes into play with this corporate nonsense is how it affects the middle class. I look at my job as being typical for someone in that rapidly fading demographic. I make a good living at it, but I am not going to be dining with Bill Gates anytime soon; not that I would even want too. I mean every time you click using his operating system it asks you "are you sure, Windows needs your permission?" It questions you, like it's trying to plant the seeds of doubt and I wonder is the Operating System asking you for permission or is it really Bill Gates, giving you permission? Anyways, with regards to the "middle class" the amount of jobs out there that fall into that category are dying off. There are many reasons for this, but the one I am highlighting here: the sheer incompetence, ineptitude and the who knows what of how major companies are really run?

Tuesday September 18, 2012

If you recall back a few chapters an entry dated Wednesday August 3, 2011. I referenced a meeting with our director stemming from a departing field tech who carpet bombed the company with an email blasting a manager. GUESS WHAT! I just had a conversation with a co-worker.

He informed it was our current manger that was the origin of all the upheaval. I am stunned, yet it all makes sense now.

I have heard from the day I hired on about how fucked up this market is and it was because of the manager. I was warned from every tech in my old market about coming here. Even my old manager made very negative comments about the current manager and that is huge! I truly believe there is something deviant going on between the director whom we met and who insists on keeping him. There was a mass exodus of really good techs do to my current manager's arrival and since then this is repeatedly been one of the worst markets in the country going on a couple of years. That's one of the reasons they asked me to come here. If it was you or me managing we would have been fired long ago.

Thursday, June 23, 2011 8:00PM

I just received a ticket for a Charlotte site. I guess I will accept it and move it to "waiting internal for no site access." That's part of the ticketing system metrics? I do not understand why they do this. I should be able to reject it but they won't allow you? Someone in the Charlotte market should be handling this issue. I wish my manager would call and say, "Go to Charlotte." However, now he is all of the sudden concerned about overtime? It really irks me to hear him moan about OT and money. If they constantly need us to go to Charlotte, then Charlotte needs to hire more techs. Very simple, but once again this puts me in an awkward position. Do I blow it off? Only to hear, "Why didn't you go to Charlotte?", or do I go? Then I will hear, "Man you really didn't need to go to Charlotte." Furthermore, they gave me an hour and a half for a ticket and it's an hour ride each way.

Friday, June 24, 2011 8:20AM

This is a continuation from above entry: I just got back from the Charlotte market. We have some really nice web based apps that are very useful for troubleshooting. One is what the RF guys use for network design and development. I am very much the novice, but I can look at it and extract some basics. I waited an hour or two, but it looked like all the tickets were in that market. In my efforts to be a team player I went to the Charlotte market. Once dispatch knew I was down there, they sent me another ticket for an LPA alarm. Thank God, I had been to this site before. There is no way I would have ever found it at 3:00 AM in the morning. I tried to reset the Amplifier but it did not work. I ended up closing the ticket unresolved. (Yes "closed…un resolved" hence the title of this chapter) I called dispatch and suggested they get a local market tech out there ASAP because he would have the part I think we needed. He said no problem and then he stated, "I just dispatch. I have no idea what you we're talking about." Gee, what a shock.

I really resent that I had to struggle with that "damned if I do, and damned if I don't" axiom about going to Charlotte that night. There were times I think my managers were walking around the office like a boat with one ore, drooling and mumbling to themselves "should I shit…or go blind?" There is a saying in the service "That's above my pay grade." He is kicking the decision-making process up the line for a particular issue or dumping it on me; just in case he needs to throw me under the bus. In my work, my manager is way above my pay grade and it is their fucking job to make decisions and to give me direction when I need it. And there is dispatch who openly admits he has no clue what I do and yet he is "managing" my tickets! How does that happen?

As you have gathered by now, this happened an awful lot in my work. From a strictly dollar and cents point of view, it had to cost the company millions. There were many times I felt like myself and others were not deployed in any logical way. That has to lead to problems throughout the network and I cannot imagine the customers were happy. And unhappy customers have an easy solution to that problem: they switch to another company that can meet their needs.

It also leads to unhappy employees. While management may have looked at us as just a software application, low morale is not conducive to a successful company over the long haul. I know some managers' philosophy is, "They are lucky to have a job" and to that I say "that's the same argument the slave holders made" Talk about being shortsighted which…brings me back to the unions?

Tuesday August 9, 2011 10:10PM

I was in training and the piece of equipment we were supposed to work and practice on never worked. It had been totally cannibalized for parts by the local techs. I cannot say I blame them - parts are very hard to come by for this equipment and I found out why.

The existing equipment in the field is ▮▮▮▮ *and that's what the training equipment was. However for the new LTE network that you hear advertised by TRACK Cellular is all Alcatel-Lucent equipment. Track is not using* ▮▮▮▮ *for the* **new network**. *So* ▮▮▮▮ **is only honoring the maintenance contract with TRACK, not with SWEDEN,** *in retaliation for not using their equipment they will not sign a contract with SWEDEN for the replacement parts even though we at SWEDEN do all of TRACK's maintenance. Not really sure what TRACK Cellular does anymore? I say this with my eyes rolled. I wonder why no one in* ▮▮▮▮ *has been told "but they're the customer" as I have had to hear* *throughout my "outsource the outsourcing" career? I am told there are sites down in the* ███████ *market and they will be down for a while. What is that sound? Oh! It is your calls dropping! We call it the "The unlimited drop plan" ...seriously we really do!*

I'm sure upper management has their office walls covered with diplomas and certificates from "leadership" courses and accolades? Any kid who has run a successful lemonade stand would roll his eyes at this entry. It almost makes you want to scream "grow up!" As the chapter title says, you cannot make this stuff up.

Tuesday October 18, 2011 8:20AM

Holy shit I am spent. I left yesterday at 4:00 PM. I just spent the last 18 hours working in a new site installation. Crane with a team of electricians comes in pulls out the old cabinet and drops in a new one. Spent hours and hours trying to get the new equipment to come up. Brought up the voice side but could not get the data side. It was dead. Tested all the circuits' turns out the data "equipment" is bad. I'm pissed because this is all new! Just came right from the manufacturer and apparently this is not the first time this has happened. The kicker is I had to drive an hour and half and almost fell asleep at the wheel coming home this morning. And I still have to order replacement parts.

Have you ever heard of Six Sigma? Here is the definition I found on the internet. **Six Sigma** is a set of techniques and tools for "process improvement." It was developed by ███████ ██ in 1986. Jack Welch made it central to his business strategy at General Electric in 1995.

Reading this definition the only word that comes to my mind is management bull shit: especially when I see Jack Welch aka Mr. "Refresh" the work force? Process improvement, really? ████████ is sending us bad equipment right from the manufacturing floor. Maybe instead of focusing on some abstract "process" and giving it a weird name they should center on the "reality" of manufacturing equipment that really works? LISTEN! Can you hear that?..exactly!

Saturday July 10, 1012 2:40 PM

Just received an email from my manager stating do not use your air card or test phones for personnel use. I almost replied and still may...but it's perfectly acceptable and expected to use our personnel phones or home internet for company use?

A famous college basketball coach, we'll call him Coach "11" once said something to the effect: "anger is ok if it used to destroy bad things." To send out an email out like this you deserve to be punched.

Friday December 2, 2011

Just got off our weekly call in, my manager informed us we have to put tape over the embroidered TRACK logo on all cold weather bibs?

Now there is an executive decision, probably coming from a "executive leadership team." I can only assume our country is now so polluted with lawyers I might run into one... a mile out in the woods...at a cell site...at 3AM? Hmm, maybe it was a lawyer in the bushes that night I heard a loud yelping and I scared someone off when I locked and loaded my 40? Darn...I could have shot a lawyer.

February 30,2013 7:20PM

Yesterday I was handed a new Samsung Galaxy S3
phone for testing the new LTE equipment that we will be
rolling out soon. Of course I have to get it "activated". My
manager suggested I go to a nearby TRACK store instead of
dealing with the enigmatic test phone data base group; so I
did! While I was waiting I ran into an old friend and we
caught up on old times.

He was a real close friend with my friend Tommy whom
had committed suicide and was filling me in on some details.
They had both started at Nortel together as software
engineers and at one point had each acquired over a million
dollars in their retirement all with Nortel stock. I told him I
recall hanging out with Tommy and thinking "wow! I am
hanging out with this guy; I guess I'm doing ok." Proud
Carolina boy grew up hand picking tobacco put himself
through college and was a damn good software engineer.
Seriously I can count on one hand the number people I have
had real respect for and he was one. We chatted about what
the fuck happened to everyone. I told him how my friend
Dave whom he was acquainted with and had killed himself
too. I have had this conservation with complete strangers all
over the country. Lost their jobs, retirement, homes, hope!
It's brutal. He told me since Nortel had folded he was now
working at a local hardware store. He said when he got let
go he elected to take his severance in bi weekly payments
instead of one lump sum as did a lot of people; it just makes
sense as he had been there 18 years. Shortly after when the
company officially filed for bankruptcy it was cut off. Talk
about get'n it with crunchy peanut butter and sand! I said
"wow! And they didn't even give you the courtesy reach
around?" Seriously I was floored when he told me that.

While we were talking the poor kid trying to get my phone activated kept coming out apologizing and said he had never encountered a situation like this; go figure? Finally after about five hours he approached me with a look of total defeat and said "I have been told if I activate that phone I will be terminated immediately." I thanked him for his efforts and I said very sarcastically "See! That's your reward for trying to do your job." He just grimaced. Mean while I wasted half a day and as usual I still do not have a functional test phone. Oh! And they're gonna pay me for this time too!

Whatever your opinion of me might be that's fine, I have a bad attitude, I can't keep a job, pick your cliché'…whatever. But there are millions and millions of trustworthy, loyal, helpful, friendly, courteous, kind, educated, unpretentious "did all the right things" Americans whose lives were decimated as a result of the Wall Street Bank debacle in 08 and I stand by calling for executions till the day I die.

Thursday September 29, 2011

1:30AM - Long night? Day? Night? It started at noon. Then the "on-call" called me and said he was getting crushed and asked if I could help him. I said, "Of course, what do you need me to do?" I was thinking this is what you call teamwork. I am not trying to get all "touchy-feely" but team work is important to me.

It was off to a scheduled T1 Augmentation that was an hour and half drive away. Remember, it is night so everything takes longer - specifically drive times. I wonder if the ticketing software has night driving as a metric? When I arrived, I realized this was going to take a while and it did. I had to tone cables and re-trace and punch wires. When I called the SO (Switch Operator) whose name is in the ticket but I did not recognize and told him I am ready to test the new circuit. He answered in a very vague and regretful tone...regretful that he even answered the phone "I am not the on call."I have become very familiar with this inflection I said, "Well who is?" and he blurted out "Pete" Again I could tell he just made it up in that split second. I never heard of a SO (Switch Op) named Pete so I said; "Do you have his number?" He said, "No, I don't!" I think I heard his wife in the back ground yell "hang up!"

He bemoaned, "I have worked 20 hours. They just say you are "on call" and you work indefinitely." I could hear the exasperation in his voice. I said, "You are preaching to the choir, I get it...its fucked up isn't." He said, "I am done for the night!" I said, "No problem; its ok we'll do it later." There was a part of me that felt relieved to hear someone else say exactly how I felt; I was not alone.

That is how dysfunctional and disorganized this organization has become. You have people making things up in desperation. I felt sorry for him...and come to think of it he was not around very long. This is a good example of the inherent evil in how management would set everyone up for failure thus always keeping the option to "refresh" you for poor performance. It was not uncommon to see someone come in and then be gone in a matter of weeks once they realized the place was fucked up as a politicians check book. And yet management thinks this is an acceptable way to run a business.

11:40PM *- Holy Shit! What an insane night. I was dispatched to two sites literally at the same time. My co-worker who was "on call" and who has been here twelve years called me. Even he is saying WTF! I was actually giving him some encouragement. I said, "You can always call me. I'm out till midnight," hoping he would not take me*

up on it. I suggested he tell dispatch to block time for sleep
because it is unsafe to drive

Again, you can hear the exhaustion in everyone's voice.
The dispatcher whom I kind of flirt with shoots me an Instant
Message "This sucks!" I get the impression they are
breathing down dispatch to squeeze even more out of us
which is beyond me because there is nothing left? It seems
every ticket is a priority 3 and I had two priority 2 tickets
today. The travel times are "always" one hour, which is
complete bullshit unless we defy the laws of physics.

This is one of those entries that illustrate why I may be a
candidate for therapy. It also makes me wonder if you can
get PTSD - post-traumatic stress disorder – from working for
this company. I want to emphasize that none of this stuff is
made up. I wrote my journal right when I got home and it
was hard because I was usually exhausted.

Chapter 17

Something to be said
for the Good Ole Days

Wednesday May 18, 2011

I got a call today from dispatch and she said I had a ticket and it was going into jeopardy. When I hear that word I just roll my eyes. Who comes up with this shit? Anyways in a very sarcastic tone I said "I'll take this ticketing system sucks for $100, Alex?" Then I said "just call me back when it goes into double jeopardy." She said ha ha, then I said OK just give me the ticket I accept it. She said "so you accept the ticket?" I said "like I have a choice!" dispatch does this so they can write in the ticket "technician has agreed to accept ticket" and it's off their hands; all part of the corporate CYA game.

It really upsets me they make travel durations line of site. I find this to be immoral and unethical plain and simple. This is done so they can misrepresent data in the SLA's. Right now I have six tickets in my queue or as "accepted." Meaning the clock is ticking on the SLA's. And I own them or the ticket is "on me" When you start to work a ticket you put it "in-progress." Normally this is done when you arrive on site. But what about if you start to trouble shoot it remotely? Is it "in progress?" Sometime we call the GNOC and go through 20 prompts to finally get a hold of someone to see if they can check the site status. Do I put the ticket "in-progress "while I am waiting on the GNOC and if they tell me the site is down do I take the ticket "out of progress" while I drive an hour and an half" then put it back "in progress" once I arrive on site? To take it back "out of progress" because I have to order parts? Then management wants to know what was going on? Why was the ticket put "in" and "out" of progress?

I have come to realize that making changes does not necessarily mean progress. My time in the telecom industry illustrated this conclusion. With all of the changes the company was constantly making, a great deal of them ended up being counter-productive. It was like the more they tried to do and "improve," the longer it took to get anything done.

All companies need to improve and grow, or they die. I think there are two distinct styles to get this done. One is the rifle approach. This is where a company looks at its operations and zeroes in on the processes that need to be changed, eliminated or god forbid even left alone. People analyze the condition and come up with an evaluation that's a given. To me this defines "management" it's what they have always done "evaluate." In my view making evaluations and carefully implementing the ones that are mutually beneficial for all parties is the concept. Then it's the best solution that becomes part of the company's operation.

Then you have the "poke and hope" approach...which TRACK used. That is where the company tries to do a whole lot of things at once and hope they hit on something that works. More commonly referred to as the "throw shit at the wall and see what sticks" strategy. Whatever you name it, this method can cause a lot of damage and you are never quite sure what does work. To me it smacks of desperation.

I am constantly amazed as I look back that a large corporation such as TRACK would constantly shoot itself in its collective foot. Many of their policies and procedures made life hell for us out in the field trying to service their equipment and it had to affect their bottom line and reputation as a company. Especially with their standing in the industry I would cringe when I saw their ad campaigns using the phrase "truly unlimited." And if you had them as a carrier you saw it firsthand! "Unlimited" calls dropping like anchors. I think if their Board of Directors and executives ever asked for an efficiency study, the results would have made for a much better company all around. What I put up with seemed epidemic throughout the company and if you had a few unbiased people visiting all of our departments, the top guns would have received a report much like this book – but without the humor and personal anecdotes. A good company would then have acted on such a report and used the rifle approach to fix what was broken, instead of continuing to break it further.

Friday May 27, 2011

I worked with my lead tech last night on a calibration. He really knows his shit. It is going to be a long year, but my goal is to start performing this myself. I wish I could spend a week just doing calibrations. Repetition is the key to learning...especially in this complex industry. You do one a month and it's like starting over every time.

Air card is finally working. This is a small USB insert that gives me network access in my truck; so I can basically do my job. I shot my manager a text thanking him. I have to admit it was a very easy day today. I checked in with dispatch and nothing was happening. I requested they put me in administrative mode. That's so the work force software can see I'm active doing "admin" work and won't automatically assign me a ticket. So if a site goes down and I am the only tech on or available guess what? Your calls will be dropping like anchors but more importantly! My time will be accounted for in the work force software? For the record I really did have admin work to do; hell I always do!

It is Memorial Day weekend. Sometimes I can't believe we've been in the longest war in history. I was in the Marines stationed in California when they blew up the barracks in Beirut. That was the first suicide bomber. I remember thinking "this is it we're going to war." Then nothing we left. 241 Americans killed. I hold Ronald Reagan personally responsible because of the ROE's. Apparently we were there as a "peace keeping force" Really? We used to say "fighting for peace is like fucking for virginity." After that I truly believed there would be no more war and yet here we are. Personally I don't have a problem with the war at all; my problem is how we conduct it. Regardless it is a very somber day and I don't feel like I should be out whooping it up.

If you compared my job to a factory worker I would be someone in "skilled trades" as opposed to being on the assembly line. Skilled trades covered people like electricians, mechanics, tool and die makers, etc. They are the type of people who make the actual machines that make a factory's products and keep everything running. Most of those folks go through a long training usually starting with apprenticeships to become experts in their fields often working in pairs for both safety and knowledge. "Two heads are better than one" Right? They are the main cogs of a very complex machine and they are paid accordingly.

That is exactly what I did with a cellular network. Although instead of a cog I was a data field in a excel spread sheet. As you can tell by now, a great deal of what I tackled was with on the job training all by myself. Hell, it was not uncommon when my documentation was flat out wrong so it really became trial and error while on site trouble shooting; with dispatch threatening to call my manager. I learned a lot fast and sometimes the lessons we're painful and costly not to mention the stress. Sometimes I would work all day with my chest a tight as a drum. Eventually I became very good at what I did, but I cannot help but wonder how much better things would have been if they were like the "good ol days" when people apprenticed and worked in pairs. Getting to know the equipment and the technology would be enough for anyone but when you throw in all of our stupid ways of getting jobs, resolving tickets incomplete, "processes" etc., you realize the staggering scope of everything. That's why I decided to keep a journal; no one would believe me.

As I mentioned before, business has a fear of unions. In their shortsightedness, they regard unions as the pinnacle of evil that will bring down their empire. In my opinion I think it's just plain pretentious and greed that will make them implode: can you say "Wall Street 2008"? But if they look at the history of unions, they will see that it is not all one-sided. One of the things some unions used to do, in conjunction with the company, was to set down guidelines for the training of employees. This ensured a solid body of employees that gave credibility to the union and good workers for the company. It is called win-win.

Monday, June 13, 2011

I got my "ping" meaning I have a ticket assigned at 6:30AM on the PDA even though my shift doesn't start until 7. I can hear the "pings" but the application doesn't work on my PDA. Fortunately, I can look the ticket up on the web application on my laptop which is a very handy utility. There is a rumor that they are going to take the web based app away because they want us to keep using the PDA...yes the PDA that never works?

There will be a big call-in meeting about the emails flying around last week about dispatch squeezing more out of our shifts. Stay tuned!

I have to submit my time in order to be paid. I have windows login, I have to go through air card login, VPN login, Corporate Home page login, and time entry application login. What are the odds of all of them working?

Now I have to fill out extensive reports and time accounting for last week's OT and on call. I currently have eleven error messages when I try to enter my time. This is complete insanity! I have a ticket for an outage right now, but I have to stay here and play DBA (Data Base Administrator) with my time entry application.

Now to fill out another OT report, which is an email to my manager documenting where I spent my over time hours; isn't that why we have the Work Force Software. So he can see where I was and what I did? I have to reboot my laptop to switch VPN's. Whoever said to outsource our field and support operations cannot conceive the magnitude of problems it causes or the money they probably loose. By the way, I am writing this on my personal laptop while my SWEDEN laptop reboots from the "BSOD." I should be going to work on an outage, but I need to get my time entered so I can get paid.

I guess there is a lot to be said for the old-fashioned time clock. Management was so intent to track every moment of my day and make sure there was some metric to generate data, that they seemed to forget just how much time and money I wasted entering data for all those damn reports. For most of us in the trucks, this ordeal was similar to being told to go in front of a firing squad, but first make sure you open a trouble ticket so you can clean and load all the guns that were going to be used on you. And be sure dispatch blocks your time in the work force software under "execution" and use the code for terminated not deceased. Otherwise you won't get paid?

This illustrates the point I want to make with the chapter title. Life was not so complicated years ago. I think because of all of our technology, relatively simple tasks became more complex. It is an unintended consequence of the Information Age? Instead of logging in our hours of work, management decided they could make us report every little nuance of our job. Whether they used this data or not is anybody's guess. It is like they did not even think about certain reports until they discovered they could create them.

You would think they could just pull our hours straight from the work force software right? Instead, it was like the end of the TV show Get Smart where he goes through all those security doors and gadgets only to have the door close on his nose. Getting paid should not be looked forward to as if you were visiting the dentist every week!

Thursday August 25, 2011 6:40AM

Last night was relatively easy - just some drive testing. I drove around a site and made calls and they did not drop. I checked RF power readings and dialed my other phones to see if the calls went through and they did.

The second site I went to was hard to find. This was probably the most difficult site to locate since I have been working. The directions say half-mile, make left at metal gate going into field. I can see the tower a good half mile away. Remember, it is night and there are gates and fields all over. I pull in, jump out, reach around to undo the small chain at the gate, and ZAP! It was an electric fence. Not to be deterred, I drive up and that is not it. Some of these access roads are people's drives ways and I have to go right by their homes at 2 or3 am. I always turn on my cherry tops for no other reason than it looks important, and so hopefully I won't get shot. But if it is not the right road, then I have to turn around. All the while, the truck starts beeping when I'm in reverse.

Then I went into the office and tried to catch up on admin stuff and work with my new laptop. Regarding the new laptops, in my opinion, they have incapacitated us with security. I am technically sound, and I cannot begin to explain it. We are not working on nuclear weapons, just cellular networks that the customer pays to be up and functioning. Without a doubt, you need security policies and procedures, but they are paralyzing us. It would be like hiring someone to remodel the interior of your home and then say to them, "but I can't let you in, but you still need to fix my house."

Manager called me and it looks like I am relocating to the Raleigh market. All I have heard is how screwed up that market is and it is one of the worst in the country and the manager is an idiot and I am going to hate it. Not sure what to think?

Looking back, this was not a great day. Trying to get to a tower and finding out I was being transferred to a god-awful location is bad enough. The point I want to make for this chapter, though, is the ridiculous security you have to wade through to work our laptops. As you know by now, our laptops were our most important tool in getting our work done.

I wish I kept a log of the time I wasted trying to get into my laptop, submitting my time, and all of those other procedures that had nothing to do with my job. In fact, if the entire company did that and you added up those results, it would be an amount where TRACK may actually say, "Uh, Houston, we have a problem here."

Friday March 9, 2012 1:20AM

I found out one of the RF engineers in my old market was let go. He was super cool. I used to sit in his office and ask stupid questions and he would explain things to me. They are letting RF engineers go I can't believe it? That's means there is only one left for the whole market. I also found out in my old market that a switch tech whom I worked with was just let go. He was brought back a few years ago. So they fire this guy, bring him back only to fire him again If this not a call to union I do not know what is.

The SO (switch operator) mentioned another email about ticket backlogs. Basically our manager harassing or threatening us about them after they keep letting more people go? I told him flat out; I just do not care anymore I am broken, he said he felt the same. He said he just can't keep working twenty hours a day. His wife wants him to quit. This is the kind of arrogance and evil by management that is driving our country to ruin. This guy is one of the nicest people I have ever had the pleasure of working with and these cock suckers are fucking with his family because they don't want to hire more people. I cannot write anymore because I am so pissed off.

I do not think I need to elaborate on this. It sums up all the frustration and the short-sightedness of the company I worked for. No corporation is perfect, but I hope most try to make things better. I cannot help but feel we have gotten so "advanced" that we have forgotten many of the lessons of the past. In our not so distant history, companies made big profits, workers made a good salary and unions flourished, everyone felt like they were part of something good it was called middle class America. Dads came home at 5PM and dinner bells rang at 6PM. Now, all we have left are the oligarchs feeding us bullshit about "fiduciary agreements" and "my data says everything is fine." Mean while back in "reality" our nation is being dismantled into a two class society. In my opinion the evidence is the increasing memberships in Radical Islam, the Ferguson, Missouri riots and people selling "Lucys" on the streets of New York; along with the ever growing population of those who have never recovered from the great recession and have given up; isn't it interesting they just conveniently stopped counting us. *Let's see Mrs. Jones, you lost your job, you lost your retirement, you lost your savings, you lost your home, if you were married and divorced 5 times that would be fine, but we can't hire you do to our policy on low credit scores; Oh! By the way Mrs. Jones…"and you are not allowed to be angry."* Seriously…and then everyone acts so surprised because there so much violence? *"We'll just take away the guns."* Sounds a like a typical oligarch's response? I guess when another revolution breaks out we could always just embrace it as *"it's just history repeating itself…that silly history."* I heard this quote in English lit. I love it so much I have it tattooed on my arm ***"Truth is the child of time."*** ~ ***Immanuel Kant***

Chapter 18

Outsourcing, Because Someone can always do it Cheaper

Wednesday May 4, 2011

Just thinking about the concept of outsourcing: TRACK does not manufacture telecom equipment; they do not service telecom equipment. They do not own any equipment, or the towers or the networks that move data. What do they do? Talk about the "emperor has no clothes?" My question to the CEO or executives is "where should I direct my loyalty as a customer?" I can only imagine the scripted manure he or she would spew. I am rolling my eyes at the thought and as I contemplate…I find it insulting they would even try to justify it. The term "out sourcing" is basically an executive euphuism for "fuck you customer." Just ask Value Jet, Oh wait! They are no longer around… along with 105 customers and 5 employees; their all dead; but they saved money!

The subject is a big topic in today's corporate world. I realize we are a world economy, but it seems like the American worker is often forgotten about when companies try to outsource all of its manufacturing and service work with the excuse to stay competitive; and to that I say we are not talking about a Saturday afternoon football game where everyone gets to go home win or lose. As a recap, outsourcing is the act of one company contracting with another company to provide services that might otherwise be performed by in-house employees. Often the tasks that are outsourced could be performed by the company itself, the argument is there are financial advantages as the justification. Many large corporations now outsource jobs such as facilities, IT, human resources, legal, payroll, recruiting, manufacturing, travel, office administration, security, storage and inventory, shipping, sales...?

Personally I believe outsourcing is an indicator of executive desperation. It's a sure sign quality of product or customer service no longer matters. It is tantamount to "how can I save myself?" When my immediate manager would say "well they're the customer!" as justification for some bull shit I would reply "if they were really that concerned then they wouldn't have outsourced it" Not to mention "customers"... don't use contracts. There are many reasons for corporate outsourcing. The companies that provide these services are able to do the work for less money, as they do not have to provide benefits to their workers and they just pay them less. Depending on locality it may also be more affordable to outsource to companies located in different locations and countries that are near proximity to where the services need to be provided. The down side is it literally becomes a case of "outsourcing the outsourcing"; which as the phrase implies can start to make things really confusing.

There are many drawbacks to outsourcing. One of these is that it eliminates direct communication between a company and its clients. This may prevent a company from building solid relationships with their customers, and often leads to dissatisfaction on one or both sides. There is also the danger of not being able to control some aspects of the company, as outsourcing may lead to delayed communications and misinterpretations. Any sensitive information is more vulnerable, and a company may become very dependent upon it's outsource providers, which could lead to real problems. Just ask the NSA with regards to

Edward Snowden or the CIA "contractors" at Benghazi. Who are told to stand down while our Ambassador was getting killed? To their credit they said fuck following process, unfortunately it was too late. The point is our military can't even shoot somebody without permission from a JAG officer (a military lawyer). I guarantee you no one knows what the fuck do to with "outsourced" contractors. Even now they still can't get a straight answer. But look how much money somebody is saving...or making?

In the private sector we are seeing more and more corporations with massive data breaches and network hacks stemming from "third parties." Third parties GEE? I wonder what that could be in reference too; hmm... you don't mean giving "outsourced" contractors' access to your network, do you? So once again I ask corporate; "are you really saving money when you outsource?"

There is an even darker side to outsourcing. It promotes unethical and deviant behavior by absolving executives of any legal repercussions to their decisions; why do you think they are all flocking to these "right-to-work" states? Companies dispense their authority and directives while still having the means to step back and deny responsibility should anything bad happen; again something to think about when you are at 35,000 ft. As I used to say "we have all this responsibility and no authority." This is precisely how they skirt the labor laws as well as who knows what other questionable deeds? Hmm, maybe this how all those worthless subprime mortgages got wrapped into safe AAA rated securities that sunk the world economy in 2008?

The bank executives outsourced the loan departments who outsourced the mortgage departments. Who outsourced the sub-prime loans to mortgage brokers? They all used different coding schemes in their risk assessment algorithms which made the loans appear safe and low risk. NA! Just like the mob those cock suckers made loans to people they knew could never pay it back. Those fuck stains new they could just sell the loans. And let me offer a very simple solution. Any institution that issues a mortgage or loan has to keep it; problem solved.

When it comes outsourcing the talent management firms (as they now call themselves) are more like human traffickers or Cartels and now they are getting into the healthcare industry…you've been warned! *Cartel [karh-tel] noun-an international syndicate, combine, or trust formed especially to regulate prices and output in some field of business.* Have you noticed how difficult it is to get a job and if you are lucky enough to find one the odds are you will have to look for another to make ends meet. Skilled positions don't pay more than $20.00 an hour and you would be lucky to get that. The standard response "well we can only pay what the market dictates"; like the oil speculators they say this because they want you to think it's out of their control.

If we examine it closer the market dictates a higher compensation then they would have you believe. The proof is in the original purchase order or Invoice that you are never allowed to see. I know from firsthand experience often it is three times what they claim as "market demand." I'll call this a "true market rate" and for our example I'll say this position is opening at $50.00 an hour from the original requestor. Per our definition a trust is formed by the "talent firm" (sounds like something a pimp would call himself) who minimize the hourly rate. Further evidence of nefarious activity is the" firm" serves no function what so ever when it comes to implementing the prescribed task (once again sounds like a pimp to me). Their sole purpose is to demand loyalty and skim like a "street tax" off the contractors they place. In business school they call it the "pimp and hoe" correlation.

I am sure TRACK leaped onto the outsourcing bandwagon for any number of these reasons. I am not privy to all of those decisions but my suspicion is desperation. I can tell you from the grassroots level; it does make a complicated job even harder. Often on arrival to meet a customer it was a dilemma as to who I should introduce myself as... TRACK or SWEDEN? Just yesterday I might have been an employee, now you lay me off and then bring me back as an out sourced contractor for another company. It puts workers and customers at a disadvantage because it undermines and erodes the trust and amity Sometimes competition can be a distraction it's not always a benefit. You can see from the entries in this chapter, as well as others scattered throughout the book, the times I ran into trouble because of outsourcing – whether with parts or communications. Read on...

Monday May 9, 2011

I do not even know how to start. It is just a shitty day - thank God for this journal. It is cathartic. PDA with ticketing app still does not work. I have assignments but I have to call dispatch and wait! In queue; which is not to be confused with GNOC (Global Network Operations Center)?

Now to add fuel to the fire, one of the rectifiers they sent me was bad. I know because I marked it with a sharpie. They boxed it and shipped it right back. I asked someone why we do not have a parts department like an auto dealer. He said we do, "It's called UPS." Yes, they outsource their parts department to UPS and I'm trying to sign a lease for an apartment. I told the manager I work for Track but my pay stub say's Sweden.

Does anybody else think it odd that a company such as TRACK does not have its own Parts Department? As you have learned with my job, there are many different pieces that go into a cellular network. They break down and need to be maintained; it is the nature of the beast. What made life so difficult was the complicated bullshit I and everyone else had to go through to get the parts to do our job. It seems like it would have been a lot simpler if TRACK had a central place to go when we needed parts and equipment. Actually there was a time when they did! It was the parts department. But guess what? They out sourced it. I found out that the more experienced techs maintained their own parts inventory by storing them in a shelter because UPS doesn't have a clue about Cellular Network Equipment.

Thursday May 17, 2012

1:00AM – *I had to stop by office today for a meeting and we were doing the old "stand around the water cooler" discussing work issues, project management or lack thereof, upper management, and my manger said, "The executives don't care."*

I think I have found the inherent flaw of out sourcing. What happens is the accumulation of management while you have a decreasing number of workers or labor the problem is at some point "someone" actually has to go and perform the tangible work; personally I take pride in that. What's scary and I believe this is what is happening in healthcare. The doctors and nurses are being looked on as labor; which is why no one wants to be a doctor anymore. All while we have an accumulation of idiots sitting at desks working for a"Next gen value-add health care company" driving up our premiums with their salaries. I am sure doctors are being told they have 1.5 hours to transplant a kidney. If we're in the hospital you and I will soon become trouble tickets at the nursing station with manipulated time durations of course? And the nurses will be clicks on a mouse in some workforce application. In the end, it is you and I that are suffering; for

206

one there are fewer doctors and as is happening right now and we can't afford health insurance anymore as it all goes to insurance executives and the injury lawyers; and why we need tort reform. Its interesting health insurance companies rail and lobby against a government run healthcare system until you turn 65 when your health starts to deteriorate and you need their services then guess what! The oligarchs dump you on a Medicare...a "government run health care system?" Remember that next time you are listening to digital recordings trying to reach your doctor's office. Unbelievable I am so tried...I'm rambling...

I was definitely rambling here but no one wants to be a doctor anymore? Maybe it's a stretch but in "desperation" Healthcare exec's will start outsourcing to maintain their exorbitant salaries because of the shortage of doctors and what is scary is they can basically decide whether you live or you die! Not your doctor. That's not capitalism that's tyranny. That's really what the problem is at the VA, shortage of doctors. Why won't anyone say it? And everyone one wants free healthcare too? How about we give away free legal representation, better yet we'll cap attorney fees like Medicare does to doctors. How would you feel if everyone wanted your profession given away for free... I mean WTF? Free Banking and all insurance is $25.00 a month. My Uncle is a now retired Thoracic Surgeon, he wrote a great op-ed published in the Wall Street Journal November 19th 1992 titled fittingly :"The best care other people's money can buy" by Dr. James P. Weaver. Google it so you can get a doctors perspective.

"The first thing we do, let's kill all the lawyers." ~ Shakespeare, Henry the Sixth

9:30 AM – It was an easy night. I just checked a T1 that supposedly had errors. I spoke to someone in a NOC in Mexico. Yes, we have a GNOC (Global NOC) in India and a NOC in Mexico. I could barely understand him. It is the same problem with India. We just cannot understand their very broken English. I am not a racist or ethnocentric. If I were in China dealing with Chinese, I would learn the language. I guess they are trying, but this is not the place for it. It is the real world. Your calls going through and NOT dropping often depend on me and whom I am working with. We were trying to run head to head tests on a circuit. I hook up my test equipment and send different types signals and look for errors on the circuit; he tells me what he sees. We do this in both directions. I could tell he did not know what he was doing; the circuit tested clean on my set so I told him just close the ticket. As usual I have tickets piling up I had to get it done. Guarantee this will come back to haunt me.

When you outsource your operations to different service providers located globally, you will inevitably face one of the biggest problems in business: communication. Add to that the complex technologies and you have a recipe for failure. As you have read, this is something I had to deal with on a too regular basis. There were times when myself and other techs got so angry we just hung up. It was that bad.

Out sourcing really rears its ugly head when it came to field repairs and getting equipment from vendors. First of all I'm out sourced, and I need a BDA (Bi-Directional Amplifier) made by ACME telecomm but they discontinued it. The equipment is still out there in use so it has been out sourced to a national vendor who in turn out sourced it to a local company. We all have different processes, managers, applications, database codes and systems none of which are compatible or integrated. We still need to get the part shipped and installed. Add the customer or the person with the original problem who I'm dealing with directly and... (I'd be willing to bet my left nut is...you guessed it!): along with their systems. One group may be using Oracle and another Microsoft. I still have to contact shipping who has no idea what I am even talking about when I mention the part...because? Add time zones and cultural rituals, security policies, coding standards, exchange rates...forget it! It would be comical except people's lively hoods are involved and oh yea! Remember SLA's?

Wednesday September 21, 2011

11:20 AM - I have been on line for almost an hour trying to square away my travel credit card for my trip to Kansas City. First, it was a half an hour to get on line to the travel web site to see if my expense had been processed. Then I have to call the credit card bank to get my login squared away because security saw I have only logged in once which was true because it was the first time; all to verify the balance due! Then I have to go on-line to my personal bank account to see if the money had been deposited. Now I have to call payroll that's been out sourced to India and try to speak to someone who cannot speak fucking English. I am livid! This is killing about two hours of my day. And now my PDA phone locks up! Guess who gets nailed with the late fees on the travel card if payments are late? I am about to say "FUCK traveling" - I am shaking I am so pissed off! One of the older seasoned techs told me he refuses to travel for this very reason. I have work to do does anyone in management remember that? I am going to bill for all of this time. I'll just tack on hours. This is what happens when you outsource every fucking thing, are you really saving money? Cause it is costing you!

Outsourcing is supposed to save money right? I recently turned down a contract position at Boeing because I was only going to get $17.00 an hour. This was because the company that contacted me was outsourced from Dell, who in turn was out sourced by Boeing. I know for a fact Boeing was probably getting billed $40 to $50 an hour hell maybe even $65 for this position. Wouldn't common sense dictate they hire someone for half of that? Look at all the money they would save even providing benefits. If I'm upper level Boeing management I want to know "who's the idiot that locked us into a contract with Dell?" That's quite a difference between $17.00 and $65.00. It reminds of the mob and all the factions with their fingers in the pie; all preaching loyalty of course?

Speaking of loyalty? It used to astound me to hear the account reps in the Human Trafficking firms fool themselves into thinking it was all about loyalty. There is no better example of this then when I transferred departments while out sourced to AT&T The account rep kept repeating "we have a working relationship...we have a working relationship." over and over again, that's all I heard. I thought "hmm great! He must know the hiring manager I'm a shoe in." When I interviewed the first thing I said to the manager rather enthusiastically was *"SO! You know Joe Smith with Systems Tek?"* he looked at me kind of puzzled and I said *"you know...Joe Smith...systems Tek?"* Again he looked at me kind of blankly and said "no I have never met him" I felt like an idiot! I did get the position but it had nothing to do with who I was out sourced with it was my skill set, that's it. After that when the reps would show up decked out like John Gotti of course, to take me to a "get-together" I mean lunch, to check up on the "job" while the bosses skimmed their monthly cut. I would tell them *"There is no loyalty to your company, DO NOT KID YOURSELF! The manager here is NOT going to turn down someone more qualified for you"* I used to get a real kick out of their response. They would look at me in utter disbelief, like I was the one that didn't get it! And then sometimes their eyes would just glaze over and they would look down. Then I would say *"just go drink the kool-aid"*, I was almost embarrassed for them, it was like they were in a cult; and we know how that usually turns out? I stand by the fact there is no justification for their existence, NONE! No different than a bunch of Mafia Capo's all in fancy suits, sliding money around taken off the backs of working people. This seems like a good place to end this chapter. In the above entry's, you see two problems I encountered with outsourcing. One is the continued circus whenever I need to order the correct part to fix something. The other is the circle jerk involved when dealing with reimbursement. Sometimes I think I could have titled my book, "Outsourcing...how corporate is modeled after organized crime"

Chapter 19

When Is Urgent Really Important?

Monday September 26, 2011

1:45PM – I am off to a great start, getting bombarded with emails about not watching some mandatory video on Customer Security policies and procedures. It arouses my suspicions because of all the secretive and continual preaching about security. I understand the need I get it! But we are not dealing with nuclear weapons. And what is almost disturbing to me is it was more of a "just don't talk about the company" instead of really addressing actual network and system security. If you ask me it smacks of the now extinct telecomm giant MCI/World Comm. If you didn't know it was one of the largest bankruptcies in corporate history where the CEO and other top executives ended up in prison.

The sign of bad management is when every directive you receive is labeled "important" or "urgent." I am not sure if it is laziness or just being inept, but it becomes like the fairy tale of the boy who cried wolf. When everything you receive is marked with "high importance" or some such tag, it becomes too difficult to take all of them seriously. What ends up happening is that I and the other technicians miss the truly important action items.

It is little things like this that speak volumes of what we had to put up with at SWEDEN/TRACK. As I have said before in this book, I am not sure if it was the lack of training (if any was provided at all) of our managers, or if this was a theme that ran throughout the company. For all I know, my managers bitched and complained and were totally frustrated by the level of direction they received from above.

It was painful working for a company that seemed to do everything wrong. As employees, we never seemed to have a concentrated voice to air our concerns. Nobody wanted to listen to us and we could have added many constructive suggestions that would have improved service repairs and probably saved the company a lot of money. And that is what gets me the most. For a corporation who wanted to make big bucks, their own inefficiency had to cost them millions of dollars a year.

I guess I was an enabler since I tended to forge ahead and take the pressure off my manager by doing what was asked – even if it was incredibly stupid and time-consuming. I can see now that by all of us just doing what we were told so we were not bitched at, we kept TRACK's weird management style going. I do not think being a good manager is rocket science. I think you need to know how to work with people and have some basic concepts in mind with what you are doing.

One thing a manager wants to do is get his or her team operating with maximum efficiency. This focuses on how a business is organized, the power structure between management and employees, and the division of labor within a company. This is where a company should ask, "How should the work of our company be divided for maximum efficiency?" Organizational philosophies also specify a clear chain of responsibility. For example, the bureaucratic management style is a tiered system of management that organizes a company into specific sets of responsibilities. It divides responsibilities between managers, each with their own division of employees who work as subordinates under their manager.

Management should also be adept at motivating employees, not demoralizing them. Motivating focuses on methods to inspire employees to improve performance, accept personal responsibility for their work, and work toward the overall success of their company. Motivational philosophies seek to develop a work environment that promotes strong employee-driven ideals. As an example, the goal-work philosophy holds that if employees are given high goals and the knowledge of how to reach those goals, they can improve their performance and work to achieve those high goals.

Our motivation was mainly the "do this or else we are going to call your mother".

You also want management to have your back and to be there when a crisis arises. Companies use crisis management techniques when something goes wrong in their business. These concepts focus on identifying potential dangers, planning for those dangers, and responding to them with a clear goal once the problem occurs. They begin with a careful assessment of potential dangers by assessing them and suggesting methods for reducing the impact of future dangers. They then provide crisis-reaction strategies that respond to immediate dangers once they have occurred.

I felt like TRACK responded to problems and emergencies more with the "close the barn door after the horses fled" mentality. There were any number of reasons they did things this way: lack of foresight, lack of money, lack of concern, the quantification disconnect, etc. Whatever the reasons, TRACK/SWEDEN's management style left many of us burned out and disillusioned.

Monday September 26, 2011

10:45PM - Right off the top I am getting hammered with emails and phone calls about completing an audit and inventory about the site we installed a few weeks ago. I fired off an email stating, "Has anybody looked into why we received the cabinet wired incorrectly from the manufacturer which subsequently started this whole problem." Someone fires back, "Why is this related to an audit?" I said, "Because I had to troubleshoot it for hours and I did not have the time to complete the audit." I recall the switch operator stating, "This is not the first time this has happened with cabinets arriving wired incorrectly from the manufacturer…who supposedly came up with "Six Sigma manufacturing process?"

I would think faulty-wired equipment is more important than an audit. As a manger, the first thing I would say when I am asked about an audit that did not get completed is "We didn't get it done because they were too busy troubleshooting an incorrectly wired cabinet that arrived from the manufacturer." This is a perfect opportunity to get the problem addressed. Instead, nothing is going to happen. Somewhere they are installing new cabinets that are wired incorrectly from the manufacturer to a site that will be down that much longer ; remember that next time your call drops.

I had a couple of sites with dropped calls on all sectors which I suspect means configuration files are corrupted. I called the SO (switch operator) and we both agreed he would do a download later and not take the site down at peak usage hours. I hope to eventually get access to the server or switch so I can make this fix myself.

I had a router fan alarm I was praying was bogus. I cleared it and it never came back. That would have been a pain in the ass, not to mention the hours to do it.

The last site had drops, but I checked the call volume and it was off the scale. This site processed 27,000 calls in a day which is some insane number. I tested the T1's and test-drove the site. I could see in the stats that the drops were during high usage times, which is usually between 5PM and 7PM. What a surprise! I put in the notes what I did and how I suspected the drops are due to high capacity and call volume. I did not resolve the ticket. I left it open and had it sent to RF engineering to verify.

I constantly ran into situations where management suffered from "Cranial Rectumicitis" or "head up the ass." You know that definition of insanity that says it is doing the same thing over and over again while expecting a different result? Well, when you continue to install faulty equipment like the badly wired cabinet I talk about is a great example. Why would you keep putting in bad equipment that requires you to go in and fix it? This is also a good indication of misplaced priorities. If you are more worried about your equipment audit and not the successful functioning of said equipment, then you pretty much deserve everything you get from disgruntled customers who flee to the competition.

I know that being a manager in any industry can be a difficult job, but it can also be fulfilling. I have watched good and bad managers over the years from the Marines to the workplace. I think I have figured out a handful of concepts that can make anyone a successful manager. If I were still there, I would pin this list on most of the mangers' shirts.

The first thing a manager needs to do is *their* job. Managing people is not an excuse to let them do the work while the manager just looks on. Sometimes a job may involve being more strategic than hands-on, but a staff will respect a manager for doing what needs to be done and willing to pitch in like everyone else at times. Many of us have had managers who use their role as an excuse to do less or attend more meetings. It is important to get the balance right and to earn respect from the staff.

A great manager sees the positives in his or her staff and their work. Do not be one of those bosses who only see what is missing rather than what has been achieved. It is demoralizing for staff to have someone only see what they have done "wrong." Genuine and meaningful praise goes a long way. A good manager gives feedback regularly and lets the staff know that he sees the good work they do.

I know that things do not always go smoothly in any workplace. If you are a manager, you must be willing to manage. Some people find it hard to set boundaries or give feedback but it is important to get over that hurdle. If a manager needs some help with this, he cannot be afraid to ask his boss for help or request training. It does not come naturally to everyone. A manager can make a work situation worse by not being clear with staff about what needs to be done. People appreciate genuine leadership. It is good to practice managing and making the tough decisions. These things get easier with practice but people will appreciate knowing their manager will take a stand and make any changes they need to make.

Letting the staff know what is going on behind the scenes, as appropriate, is very important. If something will affect a member of staff, make sure they are included in that communication. This does not mean a manager has to let the staff know everything. Sometimes keeping communications back until the correct time can save panic and needless worrying. Communicate appropriately and consistently but be aware of how communication (or lack of it) can affect the staff.

It is also okay for a manager to have fun at the job. Having fun at work can help make the work easier for everyone, forge positive relationships, and strengthen the team. There is usually room for more fun in any work environment, but if the nature of the work makes that difficult, be sure to schedule fun activities when possible. Meeting for lunch or drinks after work can help build relationships and help the team see the manager in a new light. A positive work atmosphere makes it easier to deal with challenges as they arise.

The truth is that at the end of the day, there is no one right way to be a manager. A manager has to trust himself and learn through the mistakes.

Tuesday September 27, 2011

10:20 AM - I have this fear they are going to fire me because I lip off now and then. I thought about it and my worry leads to frustration that I have volunteered to work at night and do things that other people do not want to do. Someone told me doing that's "makes you a target" but my fear is not doing anything makes you one two. Calibrations are a perfect example. There is no shame in the fact that I am new and learning. I am not afraid to ask dumb questions. Not once has anyone said, "The guy is new. He is learning and we need to cut him some slack." There are people here who have never done one. It makes no sense to me.

Along with all the Bomb Scare Instructions hanging everywhere we also had directions posted on what to do if detectives or attorneys suddenly show up. It detailed

*instructions explaining the proper response. Notify legal
since there was no security and then management. As you
may have guessed by now I am no angel but what
astounded me was it implied not to answer or to be vague
and engage in stall tactics. Reading between the lines I took
it to almost mean do not to cooperate. Now why would you
not collaborate with the police if they show up at your office?
At your home, well that's another story. What's even going
on where management believes detectives and attorneys
may unexpectedly show up? Wow!*

I guess this book is the ultimate lip off. Those with the
responsibility to make work go smoothly continually dropped
the ball. If we were a football team, our managers would be
cut for tackling their own quarterback. My lament is that it did
not have to be like this. A good job could have been a great
job, and I could have been working for a super company
enjoying my work. Yes! Enjoying my work, when was the last
time you heard someone saying that? If only executives
worked harder at having good managers who had a
deference for the labor guidelines which really correlates to
respecting employees and their families instead of
quantifying you into a dehumanizing code.

Chapter 20

The Emperor Has No Clothes

Throughout my career every now and then I would be in a meeting and management or a manager would walk in all enthusiastic and say "we're gonna do this and we're gonna do that…blah, blah, blah." "And if you flap your arms hard enough, with the right attitude, YOU WILL GET OFF THE GROUND, people!" And I understand they were just doing their job, the decisions came from way above them. Everyone would be awkwardly quite because we all knew we were going to get handed a shit sandwich and made to take a really big bite! And in that silence I would say in a soft, very bland, and with a neutral delivery *"the emperor has no clothes"* I couldn't resist! Half the people would burst out laughing and the other half would look at me very serious like. "Oh, you don't have a good attitude." I get it ok. "That's why they call it work!" I know this may be hard to believe but I really wanted to see who would even get it…and I thought it was pretty funny of course that was early in my career.

"I'm not an asshole, I'm probably one of the nicest people you have ever met, you are just pissed off because I can see through your bull shit." ~ Drinking Buddy in 1% MC

Friday September 23, 2011

1:30AM - I finished up around midnight and I received an email from my manager encouraging us to take this survey put out by our company.

I had a long talk with one of my co-workers tonight while he was helping me on a ticket. I told him I heard from another market that someone has gotten drunk and read our manager the riot act while they were on a DR (Disaster Recovery) call for a hurricane. I assumed it was another co-worker, but he said it was him. I thought that was funny. We were talking about how fucked up work is and he asked if I took the employee survey. I told him I wanted to have our manager block my time for admin in the work force software to take it. Maybe just to be petty, I admit it. But I have work to do and I do not have the luxury of sitting around taking surveys when I know it's a waste of time. Regardless, it was only ten minutes and he persuaded me to take it so I did. At the end, it had an area for comments and here is what I wrote:

First, let me say I thoroughly enjoy what I do. There are days when I am excited to get up and go to work and I am thrilled about my job. I have been in the IT industry for 20 years and this is by far the best job I have ever held.

However, I find far too often that I am completely mired down in process after process and codes and data entry, application logins, password generations and lock outs; having to generate tickets to submit for other ticketing applications. I am bombarded with Action Items, emails, bulletins and constant process changes all while trying to stay updated and current on the ever-evolving complex systems we support. I understand the sense of urgency in what we do and the need for documentation, coding, and security. However, in my opinion it has

221

*gotten out of control and is hurting us. It detracts from
our ability to perform our prescribed duties and respond
to the needs of our customers as well as having a
negative impact on morale. Finally, I do not believe it is
practical to try and automate unscheduled maintenance
because there are just too many unknown variables.
Every site visit and ticket is unique which is why I like
fieldwork. Thank you for taking the time to read this and
allowing me to voice my opinion.*

*I chickened out of putting it in the survey because it is
futile. I think it is my whole book in one paragraph. First, they
would have known it was me, and second I am not going to
change anything. Spilling my guts will not have any impact in
the accounting department. So, I answered the 20 questions
and left the comment section blank. I hope this is read some
day when my book gets published.*

I would have loved to know if they actually took the
results of those surveys and acted on them. For all I know
this was something else the company created to create the
illusion of caring about the employees. After all, most of
their actions and communications did not reflect it. Come to
think of it, I now wonder if David Copperfield was really the
CEO of TRACK. With all of the misdirection and distractions
that came from the ones running the company, TRACK
could have performed in Vegas as one of the greatest
illusion shows of all time.

In my time in the telecom industry, the corporate
mentality seemed more akin to three-card Monte. They
would continually send out babbling emails to supposedly
answer questions to problems their own "processes" created
or reshuffle the management deck to keep us off balance.

The funny thing is that "corporate realignment" has been a problem for a long time. I am not exaggerating here. This passage below was pinned to a cube wall when I worked at Nortel in the early nineties. It made such an impression on me that I immediately asked the occupant if I could make a copy. I have held on to it for all these years. At the time, Nortel was one of the top telecommunication companies in the world. I even talked my mother into buying their stock as part of her retirement portfolio. They employed around 70,000 people in what was a thriving Research Triangle Park in North Carolina. They ended up filing for bankruptcy. The quote I found in the cubicle could have been their epitaph:

"We trained hard---But it seemed that every time we were beginning to form up into teams, we would be reorganized. We tend to meet any new situation by reorganizing, and a wonderful method it can be for creating the illusion of progress while producing confusion, inefficiency and demoralization." ~ Petronius 65 A.D.

You know that famous saying from the Dept of Redundancy: "Those who do not learn from history are doomed to repeat it." That is the motto for today's corporate America and it occurred to me as I read this; our "elections" are just like the "reorganizations" that *Petronius* speaks of, wow! It all makes sense now.

I am going to close this chapter out a little differently. As I alluded to, organizational changes at work were harder to keep track of than a politician's promises. I would receive emails daily of Organizational Announcements. I present a small sample here of what we had to read and try to make sense of. It was the job titles that made me roll my eyes hence the name of this chapter. They are all real, but the names have been changed to protect the guilty.

Monday September, 19, 2011 12:20PM

Anita Drink
Senior VP Client Relations
STD Healthcare
A NextGen Healthcare Value-Added Support Organization

I saw this on social media and I had to include it in this chapter. This individual can probably determine whether and when you get to see a doctor...NOT YOU! And NOT YOUR DOCTOR! And it can be a matter of life and death...YOURS! There is no justification for her existence NONE! They are not saving anyone's life, if anything they hasting your demise. Personally I don't consider this to be capitalism...I believe this is tyranny.

Organization Announcement

> **Subject: Organization Announcement: ACME Customer Unit**

> **Organization Announcement**
> Effective Sept. 12, 1776 FRANK SMITH joins Nortel as Head of Marketing and Business Development for the ACME Customer Unit (CU), reporting to JOE HARRIS, FRANK has broad experience from the ICT industry. In this new role, he will focus on marketing initiatives and business development activities within the ACME CU (customer unit)

Business Development? Maybe if they weren't dropping calls like anchors they might generate some business.

224

Organizational Announcement

The following appointments are being made within the Engagement Practice organization. All three will report to **Robin Banks**, Head of Engagement Practices, and will be based **in Cognito**.

Effective February 13, **Sal Minala** is appointed Head of Connected Devices. Prior to joining ACME Telecom, Sal served in various executive leadership positions within the Porn industry in the area of Sales, Business Development, and Strategy.

Effective March 5, **Raynor Shein** is appointed Head of New Product Introduction (NPI). Shein is currently the Head of Operations for **Canwe Cheatem & Howe**

Effective April 16, **Ophelia Nads** is appointed Head of Managed Services Practice

I wonder if there is a Head of Disconnected Devices?

Organizational Announcement:

Effective immediately, **Phil MaCrackin** is appointed Head of TV & Media Management, reporting to **Hanky E. Panky**, head of Engagement Practices, Macrackin joins ACME with more than 20 years of media and cable experience, most recently with Nortel in East Ja-Bip.

Also effective immediately, **Kay O'Pectate** joins Engagement Practices and is appointed Principal Solutions Consultant, also reporting to Panky.

Organizational Announcement:

Effective immediately, **Dick Fitzwell** will join the ACME Strategy and Marketing organization, reporting to **Holden Micock** who will be responsible for the strategy domain IP Services and it's positioning into the Networked Society marketing programs.

Ben Dover will assume **Dick Fitzwell's** previous responsibilities for Brand Management & Digital, in addition to his current role as Head of Internal Communications for ACME.

Organization Announcement:

Effective May 9, 1492, **I.P.Daily** is appointed Head of Region East within Customer Unit T&A, reporting to the Head of the Customer Unit, **Alick MiDick**. Who replaces **Winsome Cash**, who has been acting in the role.

Also effective May 3, **Enzo Itgos** is appointed Head of Customer Support within Operations, reporting to the Head of Operations, **D. John Mustard** who replaces **Barb E. Cue** in his current role.

Organization Announcement:

Effective immediately, **Dick Stilhard** is appointed Director of Security, reporting to **Amanda Huggnkiss**, Head of Finance, Business & Commercial Management for Region North OZ (RNOZ).

Also effective immediately, Risk Management will reorganize and now report into Company Control. The Fleet Management organization within Risk Management will move to Strategic Sourcing, while the Environmental Health & Safety organization within Risk Management will move to Human Resources. As a result of the reorganization, the managers and their employees will now report as follows:

- o **Emma Roids**, Head of Risk Management, will report to **Dick Gazinua**, Head of Company Control
- o **Seymour Butts**, Head of Fleet Management, will report to **Suka MiDik**, Head of Strategic Supplier and Contracts Management
- o **Perry Noid**, Head of Employee Health & Safety (EH&S), will report to **Yule B. Sari**, Head of Organizational Management

Organization Announcement:

Effective Sept. 3, 1492, **Adam Baum** is appointed to the new position of Director, Profit Improvement, for Region East OZ (EAOZ), reporting to Head of Finance, Business & Commercial Management **Rona Muck**.

Organization Announcement:

The following organization leadership changes will be effective March 1, 1776:

Rachael Slur, current Head of Network Support (NS) for Wide Open Wireless, is appointed Head of Network Support for X-Mobile. In this capacity, **Slur** will report to **Clint Toris**, Head of Customer Network Support. **Toris** will participate as a member of the Executive Leadership Team. **G.I. Mister**, who previously held both the VP Project Operations and

VP Network Support roles for X-Mobile, will focus on Project Operations Moving Forward, reporting to **Marcus Absent**.

Willoughby Stingme, current Director in Service Delivery for T&A OZ, is appointed Head of Customer Network Support for KNOW Wireless. In this capacity, **Stingme** will report to **Boris Somemore** and participate as a member of **Dawson D Towel's** Executive Leadership Team.

I can see this scenario in a meeting:

"BOB, where are we on the marketing initiative?"

"Well Bill, we are getting ready to get ready to formulate a name for the strategy then we will have a meeting to form a committee and they will review it for recommendations"

"Outstanding Bob!"

My frustration lies in that I see these announcements and yet it is me and one other tech trying to support hundreds of cell sites spread out all over half the state.

Chapter 21

Automate the Automation

S ometimes my mind wanders as I'm driving from site to site: as a country that's so polluted with greed we sued American Airlines for taking down the World Trade Center I see no reason why automation couldn't evolve to this level with the current Oligarchy:

Image created by Philip Kanellopoulos .the image is available under a creative-commons license
(http://creativecommons.org/licenses/by-sa/3.0/)

Someday you will be walking along and you will receive a text. This is a message from your NextGen Healthcare Value Add Support Organization. Your phone will be deactivated in 10 minutes. Do to your molecular cell regeneration falling below reasonable and customary levels. Our software projections have calculated that it will no longer be cost effective for your remaining cells to stay active. In our efforts to better serve you and to be proactive, please report to one of our incineration depots for immediate cell disposal. If you feel this is in error please select from one of our automated appeal applications and this will generate a lawsuit on your behalf. Again, in our efforts to better serve our customers, our lawsuits have automated litigation and appeals to seamlessly integrate with your initial claim. In addition, you can select from one of our pre-authorized venders Mobile Unit and we will come to you. We strongly encourage our mobile units because they are team Green! We offer an automated bank, social security, Medicare and mortuary draft sequence once cell activity has come down to 10%. So just step in and we will handle the rest. This is a message from your NextGen Healthcare Value Added Support Organization. Your phone will be deactivated in 10 minutes.Do to your molecular cell regeneration falling below reasonable and customary levels. Our software projections have calculated that it will no longer be cost effective for your remaining cells to stay active. In our efforts to better serve you and to be proactive, please report to one of our incineration depots for immediate molecular cell disposal. If you feel this is in error please select from one of our automated appeal applications and this will generate a lawsuit on your behalf. Again, in our efforts to better serve our customers, our lawsuits...

Thursday August 4 2001 2:20PM

I just woke up, so I decided to write while I wait for a Klonopin to kick in so I can go back to sleep.

I received a call from my manager this morning about a ticket I closed the other night NTF (no trouble found). I remember it because there was no information in the ticket. It just said, "sweep the antenna lines." I told him "all it said was sweep lines" To take the site down and sweep the lines would take far more time then is allotted in the ticket. Not to mention was it voice? Data? What sector? What was the problem? I am looking for basic information in the ticket. During our conversation, my manager said, "I'm on the committee for investigating tickets that are closed with "no problem found" when apparently there is a problem and this is in my market." I thought to myself wow! The automated ticketing system now has an entire committee to intervene in the "automation?"

There is no doubt that automation is critical for any enterprise today. One of the things that made America a powerhouse economy was the automating of factories to increase output. Machines, systems, and robots can do the work quicker and more efficiently than men can if they are built and implemented properly.

Automation is like any other decision a business makes. It needs to be analyzed and carefully reviewed until whatever system you are automating works correctly. By "works correctly," I do not only mean that it functions properly, but that it actually serves the need it was intended for and makes life easier for all parties.

As you have ascertained by many of my journal writings, this was rarely the case. Our automated systems we had to work with became almost an enemy of getting anything done. Technicians often approached these systems with the mindset that we had to put up with them and outwit them in order to do our job. A heck of a way to run a company, isn't it?

Too often, I believe management would automate some aspect of the job, sit back and say, "We have nothing to worry about now let's go count our money." And that could actually happen if they thoroughly planned it out with input from workers, engineers, managers, etc. In my case what we got was a system utilized in another continent and not even applicable to the range of our cellular network.

To add misery upon misery, once an automated system was in place, management gave the system immunity to criticism from those of us that had to put into operation: even though, if you recall my director openly mocked it? To me, if you automate some facet of your work, you treat it like a pair of pliers. It is a tool. If the tool does not help you, then you discard it and find one to do the job you need. To carry this analogy further, some of the automation I had to deal with was like trying to pound cement with a wet noodle.

Friday September 30, 2011

7:30AM - Back at it! Our lead tech calls me and barks, "Are you updating the circuit database? I said, "YES, when I add a T1 or complete an augmentation I enter the new circuit ID so it is documented." He said, "It didn't show up in the web version." I checked my entry and I said, "I am looking right at it" He said "they are not supporting that web client anymore." I should have known? I called the SO (switch operator) to test a T1 install I did last night and told him it was ready. He just called me back and said he could not see it. SHIT! That means I have to go back out there.

6:30PM - As I was trouble shooting the t1 circuit my manager calls me. He is up my ass to get back and turn in some tools. I drove back to the shop and then back to the site I was working on. While there the switch tech and I were becoming concerned that it was a major component. It turned out to be a 5-cent piece of plastic – the thing you plug in to your network connection on the back of your computer.

I lost my notebook again! I ended up driving to the last two sites I was on last night to look for it. It has some good documentation and overtime hours for each site. I am really pissed at myself. I may have to come up with a good excuse to ask my manager what sites I worked for my OT report. I think I will say I lost my notebook in the move.

This entry goes from dealing with an automated database system to misplacing an old-school style notebook. There is one thing I hope you noticed in my defense. I had an incredible amount of "tools" I needed to keep track of: laptop, phone, various apps, my notebook, etc. Going to work every day was like packing for a journey across the Rocky Mountains on foot. I marvel at how some companies have a tech carry around an iPad or some such tablet, and it is all they need. Now, that is automation that makes sense...so it can be done.

My company spent millions on a Work Force Automation Application, and then they spent millions on a dispatch center, and a thousand employees to constantly correct and override it. I used to say in meetings, "The automated workforce software that constantly needs manual intervention." Somewhere, way up the corporate ladder, some over educated fool was spending millions for two business units that essentially annulled each other.

One day I was sifting through one of the innumerable company websites to get to my Time Entry app and I noticed an article titled: Virtual Visits from the Doctor coming soon. The key take away was you do not have to leave work to go to the doctor. You enter your symptoms into an application and it tells you what is wrong - an automated diagnosis I guess?

I am supposed to be delighted at the prospect of being able to stay at my desk when I have the flu? Is there an app that quantifies "contagious" and is it integrated? What about the particular flu strain? Maybe depending on the strain it calculates x amount of sick days off; but what if it mutates? I kept wondering who gets paid to come up with this stuff: again you have two techs trying to support half the state and here someone is getting paid a lot of money to come up with this impractical BS. I just want to go home because I feel like a sack of assholes. Does the fate of the free world revolve around my quantified productivity and the profit it generates?

Tuesday February 29, 2012

One of my co-workers told me about his heated argument with our manager and the imposed lunch hour that we never take. We are put in the Work Force Automation Software for a mandatory nine hours and told to call in to dispatch to request an hour for lunch. No one ever does, as it is not practical or realistic. His argument was to just put us in for 8 hours because no one stops for lunch and our manager knows it. Our manager told him a 9-hour day is mandated by HR. I told my co-worker if this is true then we should get paid for 9 hours when we take vacation and holidays since this is coming from HR and he agreed. As usual our manager is full of shit, just makes things up!

I guess if something is not quantified and entered into the system, it does not exist. It is also a convenient scapegoat for a manager who does not...or cannot...make a decision. You know, "Well, if the system does not process it, I guess you cannot do it." Problem is I'm there in reality...I can see it needs to get done. Confused yet? Welcome to my world. Automation is supposed to make the work process easier. It should not allow a manager to abdicate his decisions to a software application: it just leads to abuse like in The Milgram Experiment

Many of our automated systems needed to be tied together in some logical fashion. The problem is everyone (the vendors) are trying to set a standard. What only people in the biz like me know is that compatibility doesn't work because it doesn't make any money. "Incompatibility" is what drives the industry because if you have or "own" the standard that everyone else needs, guess what? You make all the money! To be fair I'm not saying it's good or bad it's just a reality of business. I will tell you from a support and maintenance perspective it just compounds all the complexities you are all ready dealing with when it comes to trouble shooting hardware and software applications. All the more reason no one has any business putting time constraints or "durations" into trouble tickets or work orders.

At some point you may need people to just think through our complex system of doing things in order to simplify it and the United States Navy is a perfect example.

The Navy of all places has a grasp on when not to "automate" the shit out of everything and they call it the Ouija Board. Believe it or not your billion dollar aircraft carriers they track all the aircraft by "human beings" moving pieces around on a table because it is more efficient than some type of automation or application.

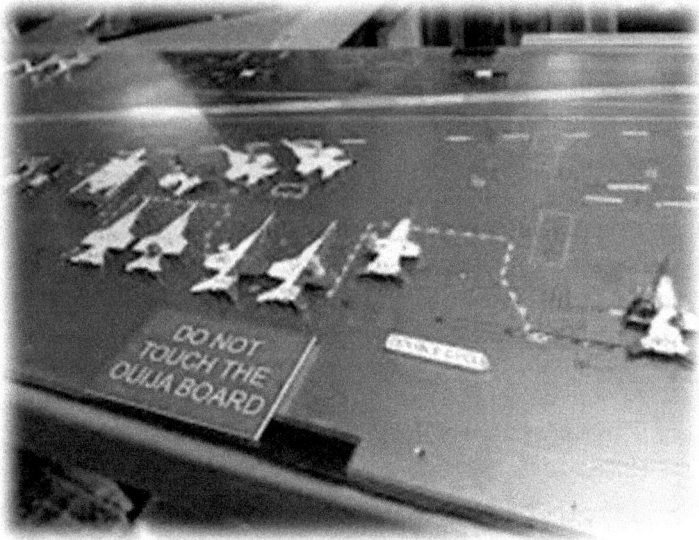

The Navy's high tech Ouija board, their "automated" way of tracking aircraft on a carrier.

I understand the benefits of automation. We live in remarkable times and, without a doubt, it is a vital tool in any business function. But management becomes so immersed in what I call "automating the automation" to get the bottom line to go up, they depart reality, like in 2008 and another good argument for the unions, just sayin'.

So when the mobile incinerating units show up at your door for a low molecular activity alarm detected by your Smart Home, what do you do? You cannot call the police because local government has them out sourced and they will be standing next to the mobile units repeating "it's the law, it's the law!" And…they integrated their database with the Incinerator Vendors who have automatic phone deactivation with the telecomm companies so your phone will have been cut off and your number automatically reassigned. But look how much money everyone is saving!

From the consumer perspective automation is being used to essentially rob us. They can't steal your money, but thanks to automation, they can steal your valuable time and your time is their money. This is accomplished by having you listen to digital recordings of "due to higher call volume your call will be answered in the order it was received." Higher call volume because they only hired one person to answer the phones. Another way they steal your time is making you wait in the "self" checkout line because they only have two clerks working the twenty checkout stations. And the one that infuriates me the most is "for faster service go to our web site" which translates to "YOU" go to our web site and "YOU" do all of our work! So if you think about the last two scenarios...they have "automated" you.

Chapter 22

Headed to a Showdown

Saturday September 22, 2012 3:00AM

I just finished a 15-day run. I am cooked. I have not written in a while as you can see. I need to start writing again. I am so, so close to quitting. I keep having this vision of walking in and beating my manager. It is all I think about. I have over 1000 hour's year-to-date of overtime. I cannot escape the anger and frustration. I billed 40 hours of OT last week. I have contacted HR, but they naturally said they want something in writing. She called it a summary of concerns, which I have been working on.

I have heard through the grapevine that there are accusations flying between TRACK and SWEDEN management. It is alleged that TRACK misrepresented themselves before SWEDEN signed a contract. My co-worker substantiated this as he told me they stopped all overtime a year prior to being "sold"…selling people, I thought that ended with the civil war?… while they were in contract negotiations. The culture of deceit and deviance in this company is off the scale. The fact that they try to market themselves as "truly unlimited" says it all. To me it smacks of World Com.

When I was in college, I had a English Literature Course. I will never forget my professor's name. It was Dr. Hester and the little prick failed me. I say that with all due respect because ironically it was the best class I had in college and come to think of it I believe he really did have his doctorate from "thee" Oxford University in England. I ended up retaking the course and got a B. What struck me were his lectures on the religious connotations of the various characters and storylines that at times were so intense it was like a southern revival. Sometimes I would stumble out of class holding my chest and panting, "Where's my bible! Hallelujah! I see the light...TAKE -ME – TO - THE- RIVER!" I'm kidding of course and for the record I am not a religious man. In fact I have recently come to the conclusion I am an atheist. But the driving theme for almost all of Old English Literature was based on the Church or Christianity's idea of good and evil. What made it my favorite course and has since shaped my view of the world was the perception of evil and how it was taught to the pagans. They accomplished this by equating "evil" with irrational acts of selfishness and or a denial of "fact" or "reality" It was conveyed through characters that had no sense of "truth" and no justification for their actions that would inevitably cause you harm. The epic poem Beowulf which is one of my favorites is a really good example. Even today this idea is still applicable in TV shows, movies, video games, storytelling, as well as the real world; just turn on the news.

That describes corporate and management. Flagrant lies replaced facts; irrational processes forced upon us with no regard for health or safety, all under the guise of concern. Complete denial of reality and facts easily perpetuated because we weren't even considered to be real people as we were out sourced and quantified taking orders from software; machines. When I was new to the team, per my request, I was put on nights because I am vampire; the good kind! My manger approached me and said, "Ok I'm putting you on the night shift." Without hesitation and knowing there was a concern for over time I said, *"Cool, and you can just put me in the system (aka the Work Force Software) for eight hours because you know I can't stop for a lunch."* I said this in a very casual off the cuff delivery as matter of fact: because it was! It was truly unsettling to see his reaction. He knew I did not stop for lunch - nobody did! And in my case where would I stop at 2AM? In an instant he became almost mechanical I recall being a little un-nerved because his eyes glazed over his head tilted. I was so mesmerized by his reaction that I do not recall the conversation after that. I almost felt sorry for him. Here was someone departing reality right in front of me. He just couldn't say "yes" and he couldn't say "no" he just sat there mumbling. *He was stuck because he didn't make you skip lunch it was the system...it was the software!*

To be fair we were paid for OT but that's not the point. If you really wanted to take an hour for lunch, we were instructed to call dispatch and request to be blocked out. Of course dispatch would say "you need manager approval." Hell, you would burn up an hour calling dispatch and sitting in queue going through the process of requesting an hour, so you did not bother. The real point of contention here is my manager couldn't face the "reality" the "FACT" that he was denying me an hour for lunch. It was the software that forced you to skip lunch and work 15 shifts not him? And that's *what blew his mind...literally!*

It was like a 21st century Milgram Experiment where someone justifies inflicting pain and suffering on a subject by blaming their superiors the old "I'm just following orders" excuse. It was designed after WWII as an experiment to test morality; which if applied to my manager he failed along with the rest of corporate...with flying colors. The only difference from the experiment and my situation was he blamed the "system". To quote him "it's not me, I just put you in the system" So he took orders from the "machines" too: sounds very Orwellian or "evil" doesn't it?

Thursday September 27, 2012 1:00PM

I went to Home Depot and purchased batteries and RJ45 connectors out of my own pocket. I did this and will continue to because requesting the time to be blocked out of the work force software for administrative time for expense reports is not worth the headache of asking. It's just easier to go buy what I need and be done with it. I will just tack on an extra hour on my time.

Here, instead of costing the company $10.00, they will end up paying $35. All because my manager (or the software?) refuses to acknowledge the time we need for administrative responsibilities. In this case, it is tool expenses and reconciliation report. We eat up an hour every day just getting logged in, reading our emails and tickets, doing expense reports, getting debriefed on specific issues from other techs, etc. Common sense would dictate an hour be blocked or set aside every shift. Administration is a "reality" of any occupation; it needs to be done. Every time I mention it to my manager, I got what I call "the glazed donut look."

Tuesday October 9, 2012 12:15AM

I think they fucked me out of an entire week of overtime. I was doing my time for last week and when I looked at the week, each day was for 8 hours, and that has never happened. I always have at least thirty hours OT. I know I had OT. The only time I have seen a forty hour week is when I take vacation. Hmm, maybe I took vacation or I just blacked out for a week? Nothing would surprise me. Seriously, I have no way to prove it, nor do I have the time to argue about it. It would come back on me for not entering it on time or some

241

bullshit. I am just so worn out and beat down that I do not care. I was paid, so fuck it. It just reassures my lack of faith and how dysfunctional this whole thing is, especially with regards to management, which is exactly why I'm keeping this journal.

To be fair, this could have been on me. I have had managers call me and tell me I have missed hours, they have gone in and made corrections on my behalf so that I was compensated fairly. As disgruntled as I am, it is important that I let you the reader know this could have been my fault.

Keep in mind I am connecting to a server on the other side of the world to enter my time. Between all the applications, VPN security layers, network latency, software upgrades, workload, and sheer exhaustion, it is a very real possibility that I fucked something up. Even though I entered my hours may not have been saved in the database app for a myriad of reasons.

Now that being said, let me reiterate the word "dysfunctional." My manager has to approve my time. So I have to wonder why he did not question my 40-hour week knowing I was not on vacation. My manager was a known "slack ass." That's the word dispatch would use. They also told me how incompetent he was when it came to administering the Work Force Software. I was pretty friendly with dispatch and they would tell me in detail how he constantly fucked up or fucked with ticket durations, travel times, and tech assignments- just to name a few. They would constantly have to go in and correct and adjust for his mistakes. I recall one day I happened to stop by his office, and he had the work force software up. I thought, "Wow! Look how we are virtually chained to his mouse clicks that he would indiscriminately slide around on the application interface." What really concerned me was I could see he looked as confused as a baby in topless bar. He obviously had no comprehension of his actions.

Thursday October 18, 2012 11:00AM

Holy shit! I had a huge throw down with my manager yesterday. We spent an hour on the phone yelling at each other. What lit my fuse was he said, "Well, you seem to be the only one having problems." I lost it! I said, "That's not true! You don't think we talk?" - meaning me and my fellow techs. It was really hard not to mention names in the heat of arguing. We both knew who I was talking about, but I just could not say "well so-so said this and so-so said that." It is not right. I had to keep it between me and him, and I did. I kept thinking to myself there is so much hate and discontent in this whole market. I yelled, "You know the other techs have the same problems as me!" He went off about my ticket notes. I yelled, "I am not an isolated incident, I am doing my best. That's all I can do!" I was shaking I was so upset. I said, "I have never tried so hard in such dysfunctional conditions. This ticketing system is fucked up and you know it!" I said, "I was in your office the other day with you! And it showed four tickets on me and when I went to look at my laptop in the truck I had fourteen tickets in my queue! What do you want me to do?" He yelled, "It's not going anywhere talking about the of the work force software." I thought to myself "hmm…he doesn't even deny that it's fucked up?" Then he started babbling about policy and that he makes policy. This was typical of him. He would "irrationally", almost like a child blurt things out and say things without any regard for their validity. I told him I have a document with a summary of concerns on file with a woman at HR. "I want a sit down! He said that is fine since "You need to come in for your quarterly review." This struck me as odd because it's

October and I have not had a review all year. But that's what he would do - just make shit up.

This was epic for me. Nothing like this has ever happened before. Regardless of whether you see my side or not, it gives you an idea of my work environment. There was a reason we had instructions for bomb scares hanging on clip boards all over the offices. It reminded me of my days at AT&T. What is wrong with this industry? It just begs to be unionized. Like I said, I was shaking I was so distraught I know for a fact other techs had mixed it up with him in a similar fashion. A departing tech carpet bombed the company with an email about him. I was aware of this, so I think that may have fueled my fire along with just being pushed to my limit. I really think it was him fucking up the software that caused a lot of the problems. Like the day I saw four tickets in his office and fourteen by the time I got to my truck in the parking lot. I would like to think it was incompetence. If not, then it is just evil. And that is the only word that comes to mind. But it gets better: read on!

Friday October 19, 2012   12:00PM

Wow! I don't even know how to describe my quarterly review? As I sat down, I put a digital recorder on my manager's desk and he just flipped out! He kept saying, "I have never seen this before. I have never seen this before." He was all shook up. He kept repeating over and over how he felt very uncomfortable about being recorded and I pressed him. "Why?" I asked. "Why...I think you would welcome it. That way there is no miscommunication here." In truth, I did it so he could not make-up his own bull shit like he always does. For once, he had to actually think about what he said and speak the "truth" and he just cannot do it! I love it. I leaned over and started speaking into the recorder. I stated the date and my name and his name and this freaked him out. He didn't last one minute. He said I can't talk with this recorder and started making phone calls and IMing my old manager, another rocket scientist. I know because I saw his name on the IM bar.

Soon after he said, "It's against the law." I said "What law?" He said the "law of the land." That had to come from my old manager because he's not smart enough to come up with something like that on his own. I said, "It is not hidden and I am not recording without your knowledge." He said, "Well, I don't consent to it, so it's against the law."

By now we are yelling again. I said "Oh! But it's OK to ignore the labor laws?" He starts with, "It is a right to work state. It is a right to work state." I said, "Yeah so you can hire and fire me based on the color of my skin!" And it goes without saying what part of the country this idea originated and is still so popular? But now I'm really pissed off and I yelled, "Call them up! Call 911 right now! Get them out here! Let's ask them!" I was serious too. I was thinking, "Fuck it, this job is over and I'm gone." Again I was shaking with anger. I said to get HR on the phone. If you won't let me record I want a 3rd party present. He said, "This is just a coaching session, it's just a coaching session" - more made up bull shit! I said, "I thought this was a quarterly review?"

I ended up walking out side to the parking lot. I called a friend and left him a message to come get me because I just lost my job. After about ten minutes, I walked back in and he was on the phone. He had called HR and the woman whom I had spoken to a month earlier who told me to write up a summary of concerns was on the speakerphone. She had my documentation, and we ended up spending about 5 hours going over things. He kicked right into robotic mode dismissing things like unsafe travel durations in the software and excuses…"we are aware, blah blah blah, and should be in place." And "it's the system" At one point the woman on the phone said "we'll I'm very concerned about our employees"I thought SERIOUSLY! You see people billing over 100 hours in a week? Yes one of our techs billed 104 hours in 7 days. I wanted to say "just shut the fuck up, enough!" I'm dealing with two people who might as well be in another dimension!…"what would you do?"

As you read the last passage can you see how it relates to my English professors definition of evil: a denial of facts, an absence from reality and truth? And NO! I don't have the option to just leave and find another job because it's not a free market anymore! Having people like them responsible for workers trying to make a living only to turn over the decision making process …hence "accountability" to a software application is completely "irrational" and insane. There is no business equation I ever heard of that says this is a good idea yet it is gaining in popularity among corporate executives; which makes me question their morality and another good plug for the unions. It causes untold damage to employees their families and the country and is exactly why shitty customer service is ubiquitous. I was warned about my current manager. I was told how he ran off all the good techs and was known to be an idiot. I have to think if the situation was analogous to a war zone someone would have fragged him…because it's evil.

Chapter 23

All's Bad That Ends Bad

want to emphasize again that none of my journal is fiction. It really happened. If anything, I probably downplayed some of the garbage I had to put up with and forgot the rest because it's too traumatic to think about. So what have I learned? I am going to try to summarize the lessons. I hope the reader also gets some of the same insights. While I worked in the telecom industry, I often heard enough from other people and did enough reading to know that my experience was not all that special. I would often hear similar observations and tales from people in other industries. All had the same theme…and usually started out with "you won't fucking believe this!"

Many companies in the United States make exorbitant profits and I don't believe for a vast majority their success has much to do with the "leadership skills" of their executives. I think it's still just about being received into the club and Mr. Hanauer the venture capitalist whom I quoted in my forward validates this: *"We capitalists will tell you that our increasing profits are the result of some complex economic force with the immutability and righteousness of divine law. But the truth is, it is simply a result of a difference in negotiating power. As in, we have it. And you don't."*

But in spite of how they operate. You have seen story after story in my case of management decisions that are nothing short of bewilderment and if not evil certainly irrational.

TRACK/SWEDEN, neither company seemed to rarely have one department know what another one was doing and I believe it was because they took out sourcing "off the scale." Due to this, we were constantly getting mixed signals and directives from above; like when I was dispatched to two sites at the same time. While some of my managers could not run a cemetery, there were a few I felt sorry for because they were dealing with the same ineptitude from above that I was. As the old saying goes, *"Shit rolls down hill...because all the assholes are up top"*

I have talked off and on throughout this book of how a little communication and collaboration could have gone a long way to better operations. It certainly would have made my job easier. While that would have been nice, I do not mean that is the only reason management should have had their act together. Think about it – if technicians in my position were simply paired up with an autonomous methodology instead of one person taking directions from a software application then the customers would have gotten much better service and it would have been a decent and respectable place to work. Add to this an eight hour work day and decent pay and guess what? You have the seeds of "trickledown economics." People are out stimulating the economy; if for no other reason they have the time, what a concept?

Speaking of customers, at some point in time, "you" the customer really mattered in business. Remember the old motto, "The customer is always right"? Now, the "customer" like the "employee" has been quantified to be integrated into a business model. The concept of "being right" is an intangible so it is "null", "invalid" a big "zero" because it cannot be skewed and "quantified" to create the illusion of generating revenue...or margins?

I do not believe I am exaggerating here. Look at how you are treated in daily commerce today. From health care to getting your appliances repaired think about this the next time you are listening to digital recordings when you call your doctor or "you are valued as a customer" while waiting on a third visit for a technician to hook up your CATV and internet. Better yet ask yourself, "Do the bank or insurance executives really care about the customer; what's their metric for "concern?"

Not only do many companies not care about the customer but they also discount their employees. Let's face it, the days of loyalty where you work for one company all of your life are now a history lesson. Not only does a company not care about keeping anyone for longer than necessary, they make your life so miserable that you do not want to stay. The goal of big business today is to maximize the amount of work that they can get out of a body for as little money as possible. In fact management probably has it down to a "calorie burned to cost per hour to revenue"...algorithm?

To make matters worse, they know they have the upper hand in today's economy because of the recession. You have people like me working insane amounts of over time knowing I have no prospects to leave for another job. Executives are blatantly exploiting the situation. And to those who say "oh that's just capitalism", to me its capitalism consuming...us and evolving into tyranny. *"Greed is good...for starting wars"* ~ EJ

The excuse from corporate is "we have a fiduciary agreement" to the share holders. Exactly! It's an agreement...not a law. But I'll even give them that one. No doubt share holders play a role. But to say "I have to make the most amount of money right this minute" is bull shit because as we all know the stock market can be summed up in two words, "long term!" oh yeah and "rigged"...three words.

Throughout my time in my chosen industry, a union would have given employees recourse in working with management. Rules could have been set on how much time was spent on the job, ticketing procedures, safety rules, etc. As I mentioned in a previous chapter, unions are now looked at as something that gets in the way of business and should be distained. I think this book makes a case that working conditions, though they are different, are every bit as one-sided as they were in 1900. It's funny how a country that has progressed so much in 114 years has gone backwards.

Do not get me wrong. I am for capitalism. It made our country great. However, I am not alone when I say we are slowly deteriorating as a country as the rich get richer and we become a two class nation. Do you know what the real shame of this is? The government does nothing to stop it. In fact, they pass laws (or prevent laws from passing) that keeps our current system of greed and consumption running on track. That is why I believe we now have an oligarchy.

Back in the day, you had people like President Teddy Roosevelt fighting to bust up monopolies and making life a little better for the working man. This slowly established the middle class that is the bedrock and foundation of America. This economic juggernaut fully blossomed in the 1950's through the 70's, but is diminishing. The amount of Americans who consider themselves middle class has actually weakened.

So what do our politicians do? They continue to consolidate their wealth and power further polarizing our nation; well not all of them just the ones in the oligarchy. But they cannot look past the next election, let alone where the country is going to be ten years down the road. If they read history and the people in Washington administered the law instead of everyone there trying to practice it, our elected "leaders" will see that the next logical step will be citizens with pitchforks and torches in the streets. – Or the modern equivalent such as Americans joining Islamic fighters, organized and funded protests like Ferguson Missouri and the NYC riots which were all about a man who was selling single cigarettes to get by.

As long as jobs like I had abuse the people who drive the everyday economy of the United States, the middle class is going to keep shrinking. Then the oligarchs are going to look around one day and notice that nobody, including their own workers, can afford the products or services they sell. Not to mention who will defend them from the proliferating religious extremists in the world? Talk about a big "Duh!" moment for the country and it may be here sooner rather than later. And before someone goes crying "oh he's threatening violence" No! I'm not... but history is.

The sad thing is that it does not have to be that way. Sacrificing a teeny, tiny bit of profit to pay workers a livable wage will pay off in ways much greater than the actual dollars sacrificed. Nothing I wrote about here is something that has not all ready happened. We are not talking about wholesale changes to improve the running of the company; just some one pulling their head out of their spread sheets. Or someone in a meeting brave enough to say "fuck the shareholders, let's only make nine million this year instead of ten and keep people employed."

Business used to take pride in how well it operated by more than just the bottom line. I recall my grandfather openly proud and grateful to work for General Motors. He believed they looked out for him and they did with a pension. In turn he returned it with devotion to his job and the pride of driving GM cars and making sure we did too. Today our obsession with money is like a neurosis; which is not to be confused with greed, I even see it in my own family and it's unhealthy.

We even "police" for money now. It's no longer "Protect and Serve" it is" Police and Profit." You don't arrest a man for breaking the law you arrest him for the money it will bring in. And I'm not saying it's a revolutionary idea but it has become the solitary and only concern. We are dolling out the law based purely on "metrics" and "financials." "Rights" don't generate revenue and can't be plugged onto an algorithm, so they simply don't exist in the decision making "process." And for the record I'm not saying it's not nice to have money I would never make that claim. I'm just saying I think things have gone "off the scale." Just for a second, if you can, pretend to be the "fool on the hill?" Look at this guy who calls himself "Mr. Wonderful?" Or how bad driving or "getting injured" is now advertised as the path to prosperity? And the one that kills me is having teenage sandwich makers sign non-compete clauses. It is lunacy. Maybe it's all just born out of desperation stemming from over population, I don't know; as I stated earlier it is almost like a psychosis and it's skewing our sense of reality as well as turning us into a two class nation.

I have a childhood friend, we played football together in high school and he is a great guy. He ended up getting his MBA from Harvard and as expected he is doing well. The last time we spoke he said "you can never have too much money" and without a doubt I admire his accomplishments, but I recall thinking "this is exactly why we need three branches of government" and…as I thought some more, all we needed was some menacing laughter, "eh, eh, eh", and it could have been a catch phrase for Charles Dickens character. I hate to say it but he lost some of my respect as it came across rather gluttonous.

I know all companies do not operate as depicted in Upton Sinclair's, The Jungle. You do read about ones that go out of their way to make their employees' lives better with reasonable compensation. From my experience the majority are privately held and do not have share holders. They understand that real long-range stability is better with a loyal workforce and better for the country. Too many corporations have discounted loyalty because it's not corporal. The good companies still find a way to integrate it knowing that promoting good relations with employees and having them part of the decision-making process means that they will be around when their competitors are a null field in spread sheet.

I turned my journal into a book as a small way of alerting the rest of America's employees to the deep shadows we are heading into. Some the greatest atrocities in history have been committed when people where dehumanized into numbers. Every great innovation has had some unintended consequences and making it so easy to quantify and subtract people is it for the information age? A balance can be established between the shareholders and employees or even reversed. I believe I can speak for the many when I say no one is "demanding" a hand out maybe just don't take so much and leave some at the table. It's not some radical out of this world idea. We've been there and it's called the thriving middle class; and again I suggest to the idea of the union as a check and balance for the private sector.

It will only be harder as we become more and more automated by software consequently further dividing us a nation. Although I was as an employee, how they treated me is a microcosm for what is happening to the middle class. Let me end with a quote by Senator Elizabeth Warren that really brings it all together. She said *"When 32 people can out spend 3.7 million citizens; our democracy is in real danger."*... She gets it!

Epilogue

Let me start this off with one of my favorite quotes. *"Anger is merely depression with enthusiasm"* remember that! In early March of 2013 while on site troubleshooting I received a call from my manager. He said "did you get my email?" I replied "is this a rhetorical question?" as he knows our VPN and Air cards hardly ever work. He said "you need to come in for a spot audit." I said you know I'm out here working this ticket at NC-OU812?" that everyone wants closed so badly and then jokingly I said "do I need to get a cab?" He said "no just come to the office."

When I arrived I went to the conference room across from his office and waited while he was on the phone. As I was sitting there staring in awe at the framed sign that read "Simplify the business"; you can't make this shit up. I'm thinking about the site I just left. Once again I am being pulled away from important work with no way to document it. He said "come in; let me see your laptop" I laid it on his desk and in his usual seedy, look you out of the corner of his eyes demeanor said "have a seat."

He spun around and said "Lisa are you there?" I heard a voice on the speaker phone, "yes"...I heard someone say the word "script." It was the same woman from HR whom was called to conference in when I brought a digital recorder to my managers' office last year. He picked up a piece of paper like a crier holds a scroll and started to read. All I remember hearing is "do to" and "different directions, it is in the best interest." I was stunned! I was being refreshed! For a second I thought about ripping the paper out of his hands. Despite my comment on the phone I was really surprised and pissed.

If I was a manager and tried to get rid of one of the few techs that could do calibrations my boss would say "what are you doing you can't do that?" Remember what happened to me at EDS? Seriously all egos aside I was getting work done that no else could do, why was this happening? Within a few seconds my disbelief turned to anger because it occurred to me I even gave him the opportunity to come clean as to why I was coming into the office and he still lied! I sat there reflecting on the immediate circumstances with a distant voice coming from a speaker and it hit me! Nothing has changed I am a fool for even thinking anything else. He can't speak the truth, you just cannot do it in this culture, and nobody does.

As I sat there the hardest thing was to refrain from knocking him right off his chair. It was "evil" and it would have felt so right. The only thing that saved him was I knew how much it would upset my mother. I wouldn't have even hired a lawyer. Just said "your honor John Wayne would have hit him" and enter a plea of guilty; sit in jail and write my book.

Given the situation it was very hard listening to a voice on a speaker phone explaining benefits that I will soon be losing; in fact I really didn't. I just sat there stewing about how much I enjoyed my work and how management just fucked it all up; for everybody. Endless monumental break downs of the enforced processes that we were constantly told will better serve you the customer and make our work easier. Dealing with this was far more difficult than anything I ever did technically and really it should be just the opposite. When I got up to walk out I could see my manager was trying to position himself to shake my hand; I was thinking "really?" Considering the shit he just pulled and now I am supposed to shake his hand? I can only imagine the conversions that took place to get to this point. In my head I'm visualizing knocking him out cold and telling myself "don't do it, don't do it, publish your journal and call it "Why People go on Shooting Sprees" I was shaking I felt so disrespected and angry. Was it his incompetence or arrogance I don't know but trying to shake my hand? GFY! It never happened?

While employed I never received a bad review; a verbal warning, nothing. In fact I had received a raise and bonus the year before. I guess that's why I was surprised. I thought they had to document your poor performance. I admit I was pushing it but I was a good tech. I know for a fact I was getting things done and by no means the only one having difficulties with management. I was told later right after my dismissal my co-workers were getting bitched out in a meeting about "not getting it done." Someone said "we'll you just got rid of two good technicians" he said my manager was totally silent. That meant something to me. Still given his history...why is he still there? How does this happen?

Right after they let me go I was very angry; yes I was disgruntled. I liked what I did. As I would drive around I would constantly see the sites I had serviced. I just could not help from pulling over opening the cabinets and rearranging wires and cables. It was just too easy. When I did this I would chuckle and say out loud "I wonder what the metric is for disgruntled employees" I never physically damaged anything as that would have been too obvious. I knew the inexperienced contractors they had just hired would not have a clue and it would take days if not weeks to figure it out. Once in a while my friends who had TRACK cellular would ask me if I was out dropping calls. It wasn't me but that gives you an idea of how bad their service really was. I can also tell you I was by no means the only tech they let go to do this. I stayed in touch with a few of my co-workers. Apparently it was a known problem by management and they just kept churning out pissed off and disgruntled people. In fact I had encountered the same problems when I was a tech. Cables crossed and components labeled incorrectly obviously done on purpose. At the time I didn't give it much thought but it all makes sense now. All part of managements "refresh" the workforce strategy...maybe they really had a "disgruntled employee" metric?

Against my better judgment and in frustration I paid for an attorney to look into some kind of a lawsuit. It cost me $500 all so he could tell me "it's a right to work state." Shortly after I posted my resume on line and I was immediately contacted by several recruiters. They had positions available and I was the perfect candidate. Come to find out it was for the company that just laid us off. Recruiters told me my old company had a policy of not allowing anyone to come back for two years; even as a contractor; so much for the "right to work?" The kicker was they laid us off with people working 90 hours a week and then hired a placement firm to try and find us a job? I can't wrap my head around it; who thinks this is an acceptable way to run a business?"

October 2013

So it has been six months and thanks to the Governor of NC my unemployment ran out. I am still bombarded with emails regarding positions for which I am qualified; most of them are all for my previous employer. I have to reply "Do to their policy I am not allowed back on contract for two years" I have had mixed emotions if I really wanted to get back in the business. The problem is I don't know what else I can do, I have been in IT for 20 years, and it is all I know. All I ask is to be treated with some respect and an observance of the labor guidelines...which by default goes back to "respect."

www.ingramcontent.com/pod-product-compliance
Lightning Source LLC
Chambersburg PA
CBHW060006210326
41520CB00009B/839